MW01200359

4·18·19

To Tracy,

appreciate your interest
in my family's story

all the best

D. Hns

# Life Gave Me a Chance

By
Manfred Gans

# Contents

# Acknowledgements

Many people have helped me to compose these memoirs. I want to specially thank Belden Merims who voluntarily edited the original text, Ora Gold who volunteered to set up the original computer programs and Ester Okin for doing all the technical errands.

# Foreword

When we were working on the creation of the permanent exhibition of the United States Holocaust Memorial Museum we were stumped as to how to conclude the Permanent Exhibition. How does one end a story of such import, how does one conclude telling a tale so large and so complex, so multifaceted and so monumental without diminishing its significance, without trivialization? In the end, someone recalled a seemingly long forgotten New York television show "The Naked City" and the last line of that show, which was its most enduring memory.

*"There are eight million people in this naked city, eight million stories. And this has been one of them."*

*To understand the death of six million would require six million stories – at least six million stories.*

The event now known as the Holocaust was a human event. There were millions of perpetrators, hundreds of millions enablers, six million Jewish dead and hundreds of thousands of survivors of various types—Jews who had escaped Hitler while there was time, Jews who found refuge in non-Jewish homes and hid, Jews who passed as non-Jews, Jews who had escaped to the Soviet Union, and those who had been in the ghettos and the camps, yet somehow survived. Each had quite a story to tell; each experienced many different facets of the Holocaust.

To truly face the Holocaust, we have to comprehend not only the mechanisms of destruction and the racist policies that fueled Hitler's dictatorship; we had to confront the story of its people; to the give the victims a human voice, to undo the depersonalization they experienced by personalizing the story. We opted for a film that recounted the story of many victims.

Manfred Gans has now graced us with his story and for this we must be most grateful.

His story is so very different than most who experienced Nazi tyranny.

He had the good fortune to leave in time. Separated from his parents, he spent the war years in England in conditions that while not comfortable, secure or loving were far from perilous, at least compared to those who did not leave. He was to be reunited with his parents only after the war.

And after an initial period of being considered a foreigner, indeed an enemy alien and undergoing all the distrust that such a status imposes, the British finally understood that Manfred and His Majesties Government shared a common enemy and an uncommon urgency in defeat the Nazis and brining the Thousand Year Reich to its end. Unconditional surrender was a goal that they both could share and young Manfred understood all too well how important was that defeat, how urgent it was.

In both the United States and Great Britain an effort was undertaken to train German Jewish refugees for Allied intelligence. They were recruited into elite units and trained most intensively. Their knowledge of German – the language and the culture – and of Germany – the country and its many cities, towns and hamlets – which had once been regarded as a source of suspicion soon became an invaluable asset as these men and women could speak the language, infiltrate enemy territory as advanced intelligence agents, interrogate captured prisoners of war and ultimately preside over the occupation. Manfred Gans was one of the men so chosen and so trained. From enemy alien, he became a valued member of an elite fighting unit, widely respected and deeply empowered. Of the eighty members of this unit, consisting largely of German, Austrian, Czech, and Hungarian Jews, nineteen would be killed in battle.

I will leave it to him to narrate that part of the story, but one cannot read of his post-war reunion without shedding tears, tears as a son long separated from his mother and father and tears as a parent who lives to see his son once again. Unlike the Biblical Joseph who sent for Jacob, Manfred Gans went to his parents. Perhaps he did not come as Pharaoh's Prime Minister, but as an English officer he must have seemed like a god-like figure.

Manfred was raised as a proud and observant Orthodox Jew. His account describes his travails with tradition and God. We experience the rhythm of a Jewish life that revolves around the sacred times, like Yom Kippur and Passover. We also witness the Jewish community of England during war time. This background gives the narrative a particular poignancy and offers insight into the lives of ordinary Jews – and extraordinary one such as Rabbi Alexander Altmann - during this time. We see Manfred's maturation from boyhood to adulthood, marriage and fatherhood.

This is a Holocaust story where a Jew is given power, is trained to use it, and then engages the enemy. Manfred fought back, not as a last stand, but as part of the Allied Armies. After Eleven months Hitler's hold on the Atlantic shores was broken, France, Belgium, and Holland were liberated, and the Russian armies were met halfway across Germany. Manfred participated in the liberation of his home and birthplace from

Nazi Tyranny and then played a critical part in the occupation of Germany.

He had the opportunity to face those who had persecuted him, condemned him, murdered his fellow Jews, and exiled his family from their home.

I had the good fortune to meet German Jewish men and women who served in the allied armies. When I was asked to advise Rose Lizarraga and Steven Karas, the producer and director of the movie, "About Face", which is also a narrative of German Jews in Allied Forces.

Manfred Gans story is briefly presented in the film but it is so very compelling that it leaves us wanting more. So we can only be grateful that he has now given us more.

Michael Berenbaum
Los Angeles, California

# Introduction

The collection of personal stories set out in the following pages was originally gathered for the creation of a Holocaust Education web site in Israel. The authorities charged with the creation of the web site chose four families whose histories dramatically illustrate the fate of the Jews in the Holocaust. One of these four families is our family.

Two documents led to the discovery and choice of our family: my father's diary of my parents' life in Holland after the start of Nazi Germany's occupation of Holland, and their subsequent deportation into a series of concentration camps, and my own story of my six day trip to the concentration camp of Terezin, where I found my parents in May 1945.

My two brothers, too, led significant and dramatic lives that were worth recording: my older brother left Germany for Palestine in 1935, at the ripe age of 15 and attended the Mikve Israel Agricultural Training school together with some of the young men who later became the military and political leaders of Israel. He was a member of Palmach and took one boatload of European Jewish survivors illegally from Italy to British Palestine. My younger brother later became the Agricultural Attache of Israel in London and was injured there by a letter bomb.

As I was composing the collection of stories, my aim was modified from recording for the web site, to leaving an understandable record for my grandsons; it is doubtful that I will ever have a chance "to visit these stories again".

Reliving and recording the battle experiences proved to be frightening, and gave me nightmares. In spite of our superior physical and intellectual training in Three Troop Inter Allied Commando, both we and the Commando units to which we were attached needed considerable battle experience before we felt confident that we could assess risks to keep casualties to a minimum. We were fighting the German Army, whose key elements were ideologically motivated and, above all, they had five years of battle experience.

There are many parallels between my army career and my professional career.

On the night of 5th to 6th of June, 1944, we landed in Normandy for the D-Day invasion; on the night of 5th to 6th of June, 1957, two French engineers and I and a highly skilled crew of operators started up an elevated pressure, high temperature chlorination chemical plant containing a lot of glass, quartz and impregnated carbon equipment, which had never before been tried in this type of application. I was in charge of the control room of that plant and I "sweated more blood" in 1957 than in 1944: minor operating failures could have led to substantial losses in equipment and life.

I suppose the highlight of my army career was my trip to the Terezin concentration camp, where I found my parents. The highlight of my professional career was a three-hour lecture in 1986 to a totally hostile audience in the University of Hanoi in Vietnam, to persuade the leaders of the Vietnamese Chemical Industry, on behalf of the United Nations Industrial Development Organization that they should give up doing basic research and concentrate on applied research to run their plants more efficiently.

If I ever write a book, I will want to blend these two aspects of my life. The material gathered here may be a beginning, but the task is daunting; while most people can see the drama of war, battle and military exploits, very few can understand the drama of research, development, industrialization and the dangers of operating a novel chemical process.

# The Weimar Republic, Jewish Structure.

I grew up in a picturesque, thousand-year-old, German town – Borken in Westfalia – near the Dutch frontier, a town complete with walls and moats. According to the town's records, my grandmother's ancestors had moved within the walled city in 1610, an unusual privilege for Jews. We regarded ourselves as Germans first and foremost – our father had lost a leg in World War I fighting in the German Army and was very active in the politics of the Weimar Republic.

We lived in a large, luxurious house just outside the town (Bocholterstrasse); we had two maids and a chauffeur and employed people to look after the flower and vegetable gardens.

My father's office was at the other end of town (Wilbecke). He sold textile fabrics to custom tailors and manufacturers of stylish clothing. He would be "on the road," driven in our car by his chauffeur, every weekday, while my mother, who was a full partner in the business, would spend her afternoons in the office.

Though Borken was a rural town, the trade and industrial center of fertile, well-tended farms, and though it had an extensive, highly mechanized textile industry, there was plenty of poverty and misery around us. The trauma of

1

World War I, with its tremendous casualties, beloved family members killed or seriously injured, and the trauma of defeat in that war set the pervasive mood of the public at large in our youth. Runaway inflation in the early 1920s, which impoverished the middle class, and the world economic crisis of 1928/1929, with its mass unemployment fostered crime, smuggling of goods from rich Holland and a search for radical political solutions.

Most people would not accept the defeat of World War I. They believed that Germany had been defeated by incompetent, aristocratic leadership and stabbed in the back by traitors. The argument that Germany had no ally except the shaky Austro/ Hungarian empire and that war was now fought with machines and that Germany could not match the industrial capacity of France, England and the United States was lost on them.

Militaristic discipline and heroic deeds in war were greatly admired, reinforcing the view that the German soldiers had been superior and should not have been defeated.

My parents were quietly but decidedly opposed to the prevailing political mood; they were dedicated democrats and socialists. They strongly believed that a nation should be ruled by its elected representatives, and not by aristocrats or dictators, and that government should provide education and social services for its people. They now felt that the ultimata issued by the Kaiser just before W.W. I were an excuse for an unjustified aggression based on an illusion of invincibility.

Father became the President of the local branch of the League for War Injured, War Orphans and War Widows. He ran that organization from his office, and his staff drew up, at no cost to the League members, all the necessary applications and letters to the governmental organizations. These papers were supposed to furnish rents, financial support and medical treatment. As a result, he was very popular and became the Chairman of the local branch of the Social Democratic Party, and he was eventually elected to the Town Council as a Social Democrat. Though Jews had lived in the town for almost 700 years, he was the only Jew who was ever elected to the local Town Council.

When I was growing up, the town had 8000 inhabitants, including about 25 Jewish families. There were Jewish families in all the nearby villages, some of which even had their own synagogues, but Jewish children from those villages came to the school in Borken.

We were brought up and lived in accordance with the orthodox Jewish tradition. We ate only kosher food, strictly observed Shabbath, and attended services Friday night and Saturday morning, afternoon and evening.

We started to attend the eight-grades, one-classroom Jewish Elementary School at the age of six. Apart from a good secular education, we learned to read and write biblical Hebrew, learned the prayers and worked on the translation of the Tenach (Old Testament)

The eight grades, one classroom Jewish Elementary School, undoubtedly had a profound effect on my whole life, The one and only teacher, (Mr Guensberg) who had to teach eight grades simultaneously was a brilliant, warm, good humored, superbly well educated man with an in-depth devotion to orthodox Judaism. He also was the cantor, the reader of the Torah (five books of Moses) and the preacher in our synagogue and he had to teach us to read the Torah for our Bar Mitzwa, where the congregation standards called for us to read the complete weekly portion not just one seventh of it as is the standard now in many synagogues. (The Torah scrolls from which we read have no punctuation, no vowels and no cantilation). Guensberg left Borken when I was in third grade. He emigrated to Israel before World War II and there became an important member of the Ulpan organization, which was charged to revive the Hebrew language by teaching Hebrew to all immigrants.

In Borken, Guenberg's job was taken over by Mr. Locker who was younger, but equally well educated and devoted to Jewish learning. He made us work still harder. He and his family survived the war in hiding in Holland, then immigrated into Israel, where he became the Headmaster of an orthodox High School in Tel Aviv.

Friday evening meals – after services – were invariably a festive occasion, as was the brunch after the Saturday morning service, and there were similar routines for all the festivals.

Those of us whose parents could afford it changed at the age of ten from the Jewish Elementary School to the Public High School, which, like the whole region, was predominantly Catholic. We now had to attend classes on Saturday morning, but we did not write in school on Saturday, after Bar Mitzvah we did not carry our books to school on Saturday, and attended Hebrew School in the Elementary School on Sunday morning and at least one weekday afternoon.

**Great-grandfather Abraham Gans. He gambled the family's fortune on one transport of cows from Holland to England, but the ship was wrecked in a storm. His five sons who were in business with him banned him to an island near Rotterdam (Overbeuren?) to which he retreated with two spinster nieces and a nephew. One of his sons then immigrated to the USA and became very rich. My grandfather Karl Gans decided to come to Germany to marry Amalie Windmuller, my grandmother.'**

**Grandfather, Karl Gans**
**He died in 1917, apparently from a messed up**
**hernia operation**

**Grandmother, Amalie Gans-Windmuller**
**She was accepted as a solid citizen in Borken,**
**because of the long association of her ancestors**
**with the town and its surroundings.**

**My father, his friend Leo Lamm (who eventually became my father-in-law) and two girlfriends ca 1910 In this picture the balloon is a fake, used by the photographer to attract clients.**

**The five Gans brothers. From left to right: Sally,
Ernst, Abraham, Iken and Moritz (my father) ca
1912. They were all in business together, selling
textiles. They split up after WW 1.
Originally their father had given them 100000 Marks
to set up this business but after few years he
demanded that they return that money.
Apart from the 5 sons there also were 5 daughters.**

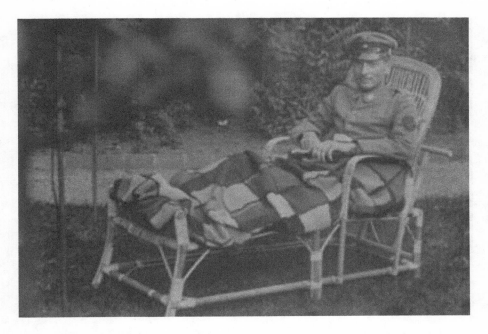

**My father, Moritz Gans, in a recuperation home, ca 1917, after loosing one leg and a lung fighting in the German Army against the Italians in Tyrol. By that time he was engaged to be married to my mother, Else Fraenkel.**

**75<sup>th</sup> birth day of grandmother Amalie Gans (1932), surrounded by <u>all</u> her sons, daughters, their spouses and their children. The only one missing from this picture was her oldest grandchild, Phillip de Leeuw. I believe his wife had just given birth.**

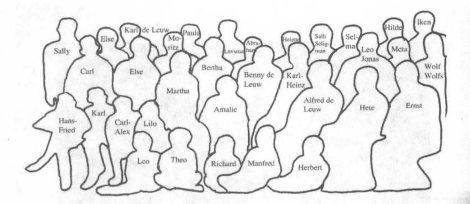

19 Familie Gans, 31.12.1932, dem 75. Geburtstag von Amalie Gans, geb. Windmüller.

Es sind Sally, Frau Else, Karl de Leuw, Paula, Levsma, ihr Mann, Helene, geb Haas, die Frau von Abraham, Abraham, Salli Seligman, seine Frau Selma, Hilde, die Frau von Iken, Iken, Carl, der Sohn von Sally, Else, ihr Mann Moritz, Berta, ihr Mann Benny de Leuw, Karl Heinz, der Sohn von Abraham, Leo Jonas, der Mann von Hete, Meta, ihr Mann Wolf Wolfs, Hans Fried, der Sohn von Abraham, Karl, der Sohn von Moritz, Carl-Alex Seligman, Lilo, die Tochter von Iken, Martha Billings, die Tochter von Selma, Alfred de Leuw, der Sohn von Berta, Hete Jonas, Ernst, Amalie, Leo, der Sohn von Sally, Theo, der Sohn von Moritz, Richard, der Sohn von Hete, Manfred, der Sohn von Moritz, Herbert, der Sohn von Hete.

# Clue to picture No. 7

13

**Grandfather Moritz Fraenkel, died in 1933. I had a very good relationship with him.**

**My parents ca 1930**

**My mother ca 1930**

**1928 First Day of School, under the chestnut tree which stood in the yard of the synagogue/Jewish elementary school/mikveh (ritual bath) complex. None of that survived the war, not even the tree. Allied bombs, not Nazi action.**

**1931 Coming home from school. Theo on the far right was then in first grade. Gershon in the middle was in the second year of high-school and I (on the far left) was in the fourth grade of the Jewish Elementary school.**

**1931 Ready for sports**
**Until 1933 we belonged to a Catholic Sports Club**

**Our house before World War II**
**The house had four balconies and a sunken bath**

**Lunch on one of the balconies of our house.**

**"Great-grandfather Avraham Gans. Here is one more story about him. At one time he got permission from the state of Prussia to import thirty cows from Holland into Germany. He used this permit to transfer thirty cows across several frontier control points, hoping that the communication between these control points was sufficiently bad to hide the multitude of transfers. But he was unexpectedly caught and the famous Prussian prime minister Fuerst Bismarck banned him from Germany. This must have meant that he could not have even come to the wedding of his son Karl when he married my grandmother. Consequently, my grandmother always preached that Bismarck was an anti-Semite."**

# The Storm

Even before 1933, as eight-year-old children, we were very much aware of the Nazi Movement. My mother's parents, Moritz and Bertha Fraenkel, lived in a small village, Voelksen near Hanover. They were the only Jews in that village. They did not try to hide this fact, though they did not believe in any organized religion; literature, operas and music were their inspiration. We frequently spent our vacation in Voelksen and played with the local children. Everyone in that village, which was overwhelmingly Protestant, while our hometown Borken was overwhelmingly Catholic, seemed to have become a convinced Nazi already in 1930, and children started to withdraw from us.

On January 31st, 1933 my mother and we three boys were having lunch in the upstairs room, which had become our living room since father's office had been moved into our house. We were listening to the news from the West Deutscher Rundfunk when the announcer casually said, "A little news item has just been dropped on my desk: President Hindenburg has appointed Adolph Hitler, the leader of the National Socialist Party, as The Chancellor (Prime Minister) of the German government." Mother was stunned. Initially, we thought she was unduly pessimistic, but the enthusiasm with which this news was greeted by most of our fellow students in the public High School soon convinced us that our lives would be changed fundamentally.

In February and March 1933, in preparation for a new national election, every town was ordered to organize torch light parades and demonstrations to show the new spirit prevailing in Germany. But in our, overwhelmingly Catholic, town there was no Hitler Youth to carry out these torchlight parades and demonstrations: the High School had to substitute for the Hitler Youth. We Jewish students just had to go along, it took two of such events before my father got us out of this extra curricular, evening duty. Just in time before the patriotic World War I songs were replaced by the more aggressive, frequently anti-Jewish, Nazi songs.

Saturday, April 1st, 1933 was the watershed event confirming that our lives had changed drastically. Hitler proclaimed that "International Jewry" was organizing a boycott against Germany and in retaliation he ordered the boycotting of all Jewish businesses in Germany. Storm Troopers were placed in front of all Jewish stores to prevent shoppers from entering. But our Jewish community was orthodox and almost all Jewish stores and businesses were normally closed on Saturday. However, we who attended the public High School had to attend classes on Saturday morning, where we did not write, clean the blackboard or do any form of work.

At about eleven o'clock that morning our classroom teacher, whose humane, anti-nationalistic views were impeccable, came to our classroom and unobtrusively told us four Jewish students to meet him in the corridor. There he said, almost in a whisper, "You know yourselves what is happening to you. You have to go home now. Here we can not guarantee your safety."

Our parents were shocked when we got home, but by Monday morning, my father had extracted from the High School principal a guarantee for the safety of all Jewish students and we went back to school, fully aware that we now were still more different.

May 1st, 1933 confirmed the rapid advance of the Nazi ideology in our school; in solidarity with the "workers", the High School participated in the May Day Demonstration. As we were being organized to march to the center of the town, we noticed that our Biology teacher was wearing on his lapel the emblem that showed that he was a fully accepted member of the Nazi Party. So much for their vaunted principle "no politics in this school".

Sometime in 1933 we Jewish students decided to "keep to ourselves" and not associate anymore with our classmates for play during the intermissions. We didn't want to wait until they would tell us to stay away from them. But when our schoolmates laboriously avoided contact with us, we had no identity crisis, though I was only eleven years old: "they", who now enthusiastically rushed into the Hitler Youth, who swallowed Hitler's ideology lock, stock and barrel, were wrong; "we" were right. "We" represented a large, proud family of Jews in a small, closely knit Jewish community, all brought up for generations in the Orthodox Jewish intellectual tradition. Sudden alienation from one's immediate surroundings, social persecution – all that was familiar: Grandfather Karl Gans had moved from nearby Holland to marry Grandmother. He had grown up with the descendents of the Jews who had been driven from magnificent Spain 400 years earlier, and Grandfather still spat every time the word "Spain" was uttered in his presence. The town contained other Jewish families whose ancestors had gone through pogroms and flight from Russia and Poland.

## Five Years of Pervasive Reeducation

Soon after the May 1st revelation that our Biology teacher was a full member of the Nazi Party, this PhD in Biology was charged with teaching the Science of Races, a "science" which was supposed to prove the racial superiority of the Germanic race and the inferiority of Blacks and Jews. Successively, as we reached the ripe old age of 15 or 16, we Jewish students were exposed to this "wisdom". My cousin Charley caught it just before he matriculated. He didn't argue, he just stamped his feet and coughed incessantly while the subject of the "Jewish Question" was being taught. The Biology teacher then complained to Charley's parents about the bad behavior of their son!

Next in line for exposure to these teachings was my brother Gershon. By that time (1935?) he went to school without any books, just carrying the two volumes of Arthur Ruppin's "Sociology of the Jews". Whatever assertions were made by the biology teacher, Gershon had the statistics to disprove them. Though by that time most of the students belonged to the Hitler Youth, they enjoyed seeing the teacher being contradicted. This situation was so embarrassing to the teacher, that in the following year, when it was the turn of my cousin Hansfried to be taught the Science of Races, the teacher offered Hansfried that he could stay away from class while the "Jewish Question" was being taught. Hansfried accepted that truce.

No such offer was made to me the following year. The teacher probably knew that I never shied away from an argument. By now all but one of my fellow students were enthusiastic members of the Hitler Youth. They growled at my defying attitudes, but they also loved to see the teacher being contradicted.

More problems: as High School students we wore fancy caps, different colors for different grades. We had to doff these caps when we met a teacher on the street, but now an order came to replace the doffing of the cap with the Hitler Salute. We refused to go along, even when some of the teachers who, secretly did not approve of the Nazi ideology, argued that the outstretched arm was now the German Salute and not necessarily the Hitler Salute.

The old "establishment" of teachers who ran the High School never became enthusiastic Nazis. The Nazi authorities must have been well aware of that fact, because eventually they brought in a teacher who had been a longtime member of the Nazi party whom they trusted to report on all the other teachers. This "trustee" was an unsavory character, an alcoholic with no depth of knowledge to teach any subject. He taught Geography to my class for one year. During that time he tried his best to ignore me: he never called on me to give an answer or a presentation and he never marked my tests. At the end of the year he gave me a "C" for the course, to save himself any arguments. Luckily, the unmarried daughter of the "trustee" got pregnant and he and his family had to move away.

A new, young Gymnastics teacher presented a much greater danger. This man was a fanatical Nazi who made sure that I never won anything in sports. There was a ruling in those days that nobody could be promoted to a higher grade without at least a passing grade in gymnastics. After just one sole exercise on the parallel bars, he announced that my performance was totally insufficient and I got an "F" in Sports and Gymnastics on my report card. Nevertheless, through the intervention of some of the teachers who knew me well, I was promoted to the next grade.

I vowed to "show them something". In those days the school year ended before the Easter vacation; that was the time for report cards and promotions. For these vacations I got myself a Jewish tutor for sports who arranged for us to use a gymnasium for Jewish clubs in Cologne. I worked with the tutor for at least two hours every day for almost two weeks, at the end of which I knew that I could outperform anyone in my grade at school in gymnastics.

## Life Must Go On

The ramifications of having to live with the pervasive teaching of the Nazi ideology did not diminish all the normal problems of a High School education. We still had to learn Latin (at times I got bad marks and I had to get a tutor), French, English, Mathematics, German Literature, Physics, Chemistry etc. etc. There were glorious summer vacations spent on the Agricultural Training Farm ran by our uncle and aunt, or spent on the beach in Holland. My younger brother, Theo, and I spent two weeks in a ski resort in Thueringen. We ate lunch and supper in a Jewish hotel, but for a number of reasons we had to hide the fact that we were Jewish in all other places.

When German society was slammed shut, our Jewish community readily, eagerly turned to Zionism, Hebrew and Jewish traditional learning. Under the guidance of the teacher of our Jewish Elementary school we became members of the youth group of the Orthodox Zionist movement and we had Hebrew lessons every afternoon except Friday.

But there also was an emphasis on learning practical skills; on my uncle's agricultural training farm we worked with the other trainees and during the winter vacation I once worked as an apprentice in a carpentry shop.

And so, my older brother left home for Palestine in 1936 at the "ripe" age of sixteen and after 5 years of hardly exchanging a word with any German classmates in High School, I left for England in the summer of 1938, relishing the thought of new adventures and the thought of a free society where I would be able to talk to anybody and everybody. Only the prospect of never again seeing the beautiful fields, forests, flatlands, mountains, towns, and villages where I had grown up occasionally filled me with pangs of sadness: the Hitler Reich would last for generations and we would never be allowed to return.

**The official picture for my barmitzvah. Used for all invitations and printed menus.**
**Already at that time I was an avid reader of newspapers.**

**Fourth year of high-school**
**Note the fancy caps we had to wear**

**1938 Theo's barmitzvah
With my father in our garden**

# Freedom and the Clouds of War

I left Germany on a Friday afternoon in July, 1938. My father took me across the frontier to his cousin in Winterswyk, Holland. On Sunday morning I traveled on alone by train to the Hook of Holland to take the night ferry to England. I cherished the adventure and the excitement; I never went to sleep, but had a chance to try out my English on two young British girls. Next morning we landed in Harwich and, as instructed, I took the train to Liverpool Street station in London.

Through a young lady from Borken, who was married to one of the Rabbi Karlebachs, my parents had made arrangements for me to live with the Jacobs family in Golders-Green, London, Mrs. Jacobs met me at the train. She was a slender, well-dressed lady, who spoke some German. She thought my suitcase was far too heavy for me alone to carry, so she insisted that we both carry it together, up and down the steps from the station to the underground. That impressed me. During the next few weeks I grew very fond of her; apart from working very hard looking after a large household, she had no hesitation in correcting my English and making suggestions on how to further my studies.

Mr. Jacobs was an insurance salesman. He had been an officer in the Jewish Legion in World War I, a part of history with which I was very familiar from my Zionist education. When he first told me about his past, I said, "You must have been together with Jabotinsky" (founder and leader of the Revisionist Party), and he made it very clear that he strongly disagreed with Jabotinsky. In British politics he was a Liberal; the newspaper we got every morning was the News Chronicle. Since I loved to read newspapers, I laboriously translated short articles from the News Chronicle and then tried to learn them by heart to improve my English. Thus my initial education in a free society was very much colored by the Liberal point of view.

Much to the chagrin of his hard-working wife, Mr. Jacobs occasionally "played hooky", spending his afternoons at the Lords Cricket Ground watching the test matches. Occasionally, we went to the movies together, a pleasant way to further improve my English. One day he asked me whether I wanted a book from the library and I requested Hitler's "Mein Kampf" in German, which I proceeded to read from cover to cover. In Germany I would not have done "them" the honor to read this bible of the Nazis, but now it was just part of being informed. It proved a good guide for what would happen in the next two years.

The Jacobs had one daughter, my age, a very lovely, well-educated young lady. We spent some good times together; she was as pleasant to be with as her parents. Also in the house lived a young, quite wealthy, Polish girl, a distant relative of the Jacobs. She spent just about every afternoon at the movies. An orphaned nephew of the Jacobs, who was an apprentice in some business, was the other permanent resident. A big household and the food was very good, though we all only ate together on Friday nights and Saturday lunchtime.

Almost all my subsequent high-powered contacts in England were the result of introductions from Mr. Jacobs.

## Student

I was supposed to stay in England for two months, then return home to start attending a Jewish High School in Berlin, but after a few weeks my parents wrote, "What would you do, if we asked you to stay in England permanently?"

I knew exactly what I wanted: try to get a high school certificate, then start working as a mechanic apprentice while continuing my studies to become an engineer in evening classes. My cousin Bernard Moch, who attended Bunce Court, a boarding school in Kent, had introduced me to the Adler-Rudel family. Mr. Adler-Rudel was a permanent official of the Jewish Agency and, on his family's advice, I decided to enlist in a tutorial college in London, a school that did nothing but prepare students for "Matric". The daughter of the Adler-Rudels, Rachel, who was a good-looking girl, joined me there, but she took the eight months course, while I had enough money only for the four-month course. Rachel's friend, who was the daughter of Arlosorof, another famous name in Zionist history, also enlisted in the tutorial college. Eventually, I also met Shertok, who, as Shareth, became the first Secretary of Foreign Affaires of Israel eight years later, at a party in the Adler-Rudel home.

"Board and lodgings" at the Jacobs was too expensive. I found a much cheaper place with a Jewish widow near the Brent subway station. From there I could still attend the Golders Green Synagogue, which was close to the Jacobs' house, and I could commute easily by subway to the tutorial college.

As I started to attend the tutorial college, Hitler's demands on Czechoslovakia became frenzied, leaving no doubt that he was willing to go to war in order to absorb the Sudeten Germans into his Reich. The attitude of the British government was that, in case of war, it would have no choice but to back Czechoslovakia. With a lot of fanfare, a puny number of antiaircraft guns were moved into

London, an organization of air-raid wardens was created, gas masks were handed out to the population, and "non-essential" people were encouraged to leave London. My landlady and her two daughters left for the countryside, and I had to look after myself, which I did not mind at all.

The infamous Munich conference was supposed to be the last chance to avoid war. At that conference, France and England agreed to let Hitler absorb the Sudetenland. The British Prime Minister, Chamberlain, returned to London waving his "peace in our times" document. In my circles nobody believed him. The reaction next Shabbat in the quite wealthy Golders Green synagogue revealed the different attitudes. Liberals like Mr. Jacobs strongly disapproved of the Munich deal, quoting the maverick, Conservative Member of Parliament, Winston Churchill, who said to Chamberlain in a House of Commons speech, "You had to choose between dishonor and war. You chose dishonor and you will get a war." The Conservative Jews pointed out that England was not ready for war and that Chamberlain had just bought time to rearm. (There was some validity to that argument). Those Jews who were adherents of the Labor party had been confirmed pacifists, and their main concern now was opposition to the reintroduction of the draft to build up the armed forces. These arguments continued to rage during the next twelve months.

Requirements for the "Matric" were so flexible that I could just concentrate on courses in English, Mathematics, Mechanics and Electricity. I did a minimum amount of work for the latter three courses and focused almost exclusively on English. I had no difficulty following the courses, but the English, which included a Shakespeare play, a poetry book, a classic novel and a rigid, systematic approach to composition and literary evaluation was a major challenge. We had not been taught such a systematic approach to German in our high school in Germany.

Four weeks before the end of the term of the tutorial college and the subsequent public "Matric" examination in the London University (by that time it was January 1939), the college reviewed my performance and predicted that I would pass the English examination, but fail in all the other subjects. Of course, no surprise to me, the results were exactly the opposite: I passed all subjects except the English.

While waiting for the results of the examination, I started to look for ways to get an apprentice job in machine repairing. I had made up my mind to continue "Matric" courses or start engineering courses by evening classes only.

During that time my uncle, Alex Moch, who was in charge of a Jewish agricultural training school in Germany (Gut Neuendorf), came to England with the idea of setting up a similar training school in England and transferring all his students and personnel from Germany to England. He asked me to be his interpreter. This proved to be a fascinating experience. Eventually, through the German Jewish Aid Committee, a number of rich people got together and created Tythrope House, near Oxford, to which Alex could transfer his students and personnel.

The membership of the committee of philanthropists which created Tythrop House presented very different points of views. The chairman was a wealthy, bachelor attorney, who operated from an office/apartment near Oxford Circle. Very often, when we went there in the morning he was still in his housecoat. Politically, he was an outspoken Communist. In contrast, the treasurer was an ultra conservative who wrote with a quill.

One Sunday we went by chauffeur-driven car to Tythrop House. The Communist chairman brought along a reporter from the Sunday Express to get some publicity for the venture. The article, which the Express published the following Sunday, was largely about me, but it did not mention any names.

## Manchester

Jobs for unskilled people like me were very hard to get. There still was a lot of unemployment in England, the German Jewish Aid Committee, through its connection to Jewish employers, was almost the only access to paid work. The offices of the Aid Committee were in Euston and life there was frantic. Most of the staff were high society Jewish ladies who worked as volunteers, and they were continuously besieged by refugees who needed jobs for themselves or for friends and family still in Germany, Austria or Czechoslovakia. I watched all these frantic efforts for almost a whole day. In the late afternoon, the lady at whose desk I had lined up (she was from the Sieff family) casually asked me, "Would you like to go to Manchester?" I agreed eagerly; decentralization of the refugee community was the only hope of finding work. A few days later I met a group of six or seven young men to take a train to Manchester.

In Manchester, we were brought into a very well run hostel for temporary residence until we could find work. There were about 50 men and women living in the hostel at any one time. Again, the ladies in charge were volunteers from well-to-do families and of course, we all had to help with cleaning and cooking. There were only two other orthodox Jews in the hostel while I was there. They came from a Chasidic community in Austria, and they persuaded me to walk with them to a Chassidic synagogue in Cheetham Hill on Saturdays, almost an hour's walk. We were always invited for lunch by one or another Chassidic family.

After a week or two, the Refugee Committee thought they had a job of interest to me. I was given the address and I was told that this was the first non-Jewish firm that had offered to help and that I was to accept whatever job and condition made available to me. I had no intention of following that advice: I was not going to accept work which did not further my potential career as an engineer.

The factory, whose co-owner-director interviewed me, was a mass producer of furniture. It was highly automated: chips were sucked off all woodworking machines to be blown into a steam generating furnace for generation of the factory's own electricity. Alternatively, the wood waste was blown into a complicated mill for producing wood flour, apparently used as a filler for plastics.

The director explained that he had a dilemma: the factory was unionized in its carpentry and furniture manufacturing departments, and there would be no job for me, even as an apprentice, in those skills. I explained that I wanted to be an engineer eventually and that the only job which interested me would be in his machine and truck repair department. It turned out that those skills were not covered by the union, so they were delighted to give me a job as a machine repair fitter.

I then explained that I was an orthodox Jew and that I would not work on Saturday and that I had to get home on Friday before sundown. All these conditions were readily agreed to. I would be on an hourly wage and I would have to clock in and out every day. "A lad who does not work, does not get paid."

I was deliriously happy. This was my first paid employment, though I made considerably less than a living wage, but the Aid Committee had promised to subsidize me initially.

After I had been working for a few days, I was told in the hostel to visit a family that would arrange for me to find a room and lodging. I made my way there by bus in the evening and was surprised and a bit embarrassed – I had hardly changed from my working clothing – to find myself in a very stately home.

That's how I came to know the Steinart family; they were regarded as the second richest Jewish family in Manchester after the Laskis, to whom I was also introduced eventually. Unbeknownst to me, the contact to the Steinarts had been made by Mr. Jacobs; Mrs. Steinhart's brother had also been an officer in the Jewish Brigade during World War I.

It was arranged that I rent a room from Mr. Steinart's stepmother, a lady who was younger than Mr. Steinart, whom his father had married in his old age. The Steinarts asked me to spend every Friday night and Shabbat dinner with them, and I regularly attended services in the Synagogue, where Mr. Steinart was the President. Some of the younger active members of the synagogue eventually became quite well known in Zionist politics and in Manchester political life. Also, the synagogue had a beautiful male choir for the services.

I relished the "dual" identity life which I led: being a member of the working class in pretty filthy circumstances all week and spending time with the very rich during the weekend. A heavy German bike, which my parents had sent me, was my sole method of transportation for commuting, attending classes in the evening, and visiting friends.

In the machine repair department we had laths, metal planers, heavy drills, welding equipment and whatever was required to repair or produce spare parts for the high-speed wood working machinery and the company's trucks and cars. I mainly worked with the chief mechanic, who was highly skilled and took great care to educate me. He had no academic training and was happy to let me do all the calculations. The mechanic in charge of car and truck repairs was similarly warm and caring.

My landlady had two other lodgers, an old man, who was retired and very set in his ways, and a German Jew about two years older than I, who worked as a carpenter and took courses to become a designer, was orthodox like me and was quite involved in the Zionist Youth movement. His name was Franz Pinczower. I was very fond of him. We remained friends for life. Passover 1939, he had me invited to his cousins, Leo and Luise Wislicki, for Seder, and that was the start of my friendship with the Wislickis, which also lasted for life.

March 1939, Hitler "absorbed" the rest of Czechoslovakia. It was now obvious that he was following his plan of expanding Germany and "pushing all the Slavic people into the Russian Raum" (space). Chamberlain, still Prime Minister of Great Britain, made a good speech on a Friday night, to which we listened while I was at the Steinarts. He even expressed concern for the Czech Jews. Everyone now agreed that war was inevitable. France and Great Britain started to negotiate with the Soviet Union to form a Great Alliance against Hitler, but Stalin was not interested. After months of negotiations, he suddenly made a pact with Hitler to divide up Poland. That was Hitler's go-ahead for the war.

All this time, I could travel freely because my parents could send me railway tickets from Germany, paid with German money, with which they found it difficult to do anything useful. There was strict currency control in Germany; anyone going abroad could not take more than ten Marks, enough to pay for two good meals. The Hitler adventures had devalued the currency to such an extent that large sums of Marks were hard to dispose of.

For the last two days of Passover and subsequent Easter holidays I went to Tythrop House, where by now my uncle, Alex Moch, and his whole family had taken residence. Of course, that Agricultural Training Center, which Alex and his staff had set up, was not kosher, and I had a tough time living on a strictly vegetarian diet without bread or flour. Alex and Erna Moch, who had been running agricultural training schools for Jews all their lives, had made up their minds to pursue another career. They had agreed to run a large farm for a British officer in Kenya. Their son Bernard, who was 16 years old, was going with them, but they could not see a way to send their daughter, Recha, to a school in Kenya. She remained in England, going to the same boarding school as my bother Teo. Recha did not like this arrangement at all, and while we were at Typthrop House she protested vehemently against it. She did not see her parents again until the sixties. By that time they had retired to Israel. Recha, who had become a nurse during the war, was married and had children. But I stayed in touch with Recha all the time, including attending her wedding in 1947.

For the after-service lunch, Shevuoth 1939, the Steinarts had invited the new Communal (Chief) Rabbi of Manchester, Dr. Alexander Altmann, and his wife, Judith. Altmann had been the Rabbi of a famous Berlin synagogue. For the lunch the dairy food was magnificent, the day was beautiful, we enjoyed the magnificent home, garden and servants of the Steinarts to the fullest. The Altmanns and I "hit it off" right away. Altmann told me that he was about to start a course on Jewish philosophy in German, in his home on Saturday afternoons. The course, based on the medieval book "El Kousari", started soon thereafter and was my first exposure to Altmann's lifelong guidance of my views on Judaism. (In the '50s Altmann became the Director of the Institute for Advanced Jewish Studies of Brandeis University, so we met regularly; particularly, because Judith Altmann, Dr Altmann's wife, and Anita, my wife, had become great friends.)

**Tythrope House Easter 1939**
**Interpreting for my uncle Alex Moch (on the left}**
**and the chairman of the Tythrope House committee**

**Rabbi Dr. Alexander Altmann**

**Professor Rabbi Altmann was a young, Orthodox rabbi in Berlin, Germany when Hitler came to power. He later became the Communal Rabbi of Manchester, England and in the '50s was appointed Professor of Jewish Philosophy and History of Ideas at Brandeis University. Recognized as a leading scholar of Jewish philosophy, theology and intellectual history he also held an honorary appointment at Harvard, the Hebrew University in Jerusalem and numerous other academic and religious institutions. His research and writing were prolific. He died in 1987.**

**Judith Altmann**
**Judith Altmann, wife of Rabbi Altmann.**

# War

To nobody's surprise, the war started on Friday September 1st, 1939. France and Great Britain had given a guarantee to Poland that they would declare war on Germany if Poland was attacked. Hitler, the eternal liar, now claimed that this guarantee had emboldened the Poles to attack Germany! On Sunday September 3rd, Great Britain and France declared war on Germany. Again, I was at the Steinart's to listen to Chamberlain's speech ("...it is the evil things we shall be fighting against, – brute force, bad faith, injustice, oppression, and persecution and against them, I am certain that the right will prevail...")

I did not own a radio, but German broadcasts could be received easily, and I made a point of listening to Hitler's speeches on my landlady's set.

Hitler marched into Poland from the west and Stalin marched into Poland from the east. They divided up Poland along a pre-negotiated demarcation line. This phase of the war lasted less than three weeks; then Hitler made his triumphal speech, in Danzig, in which he set out his program for dealing with his new territories, including "a final solution" for the Jewish problem. "Eine entgueltige Loesung der

Judenfrage". But in my opinion, (I listened to the speech), he said, "Eine aufrichtige (honest) Loesung der Judenfrage.") He was too devious to be caught with such a phrase as "final solution," though that is what he meant, or what appeared in the Goebbels' edited transcript. To the German people, Hitler always wanted to represent himself as the constructive, Wagner loving, caring intellectual. Criticism of brutalities had to be directed to his underlings.

With the outbreak of war, we German and Austrian refugees now became "enemy aliens." Tribunals were set up to examine and classify our status. Those assigned to class A were interned immediately; class B were kept under some surveillance but they were not interned immediately. Class C were given complete freedom. With all my contacts, I had no difficulty getting a C status.

Evenings and weekends, I continued to prepare myself for the Matric examination. Once a week I took private lessons for the English portion of the examination, necessitating long rides by bicycle to different parts of Manchester. In January, 1940, I again "sat" for the examination. This time I passed. My parents in Holland were delighted, as were my friends, the Steinarts. I too felt that this was a major step forward in my professional career. It was my intention to get a degree in Mechanical

Engineering in evening classes in Manchester University while continuing to work during the day. I wanted to specialize in agricultural machinery to eventually emigrate to Israel.

In the spring of 1940, mobilization got into its full stride in Great Britain: the war industry recruited additional shifts to work day and night. Young men were drafted into the army, navy and air force; women replaced men in many industries. Eventually, the country was mobilized to a degree which has not been experienced anywhere before or since.

Jobs were now readily available and I decided to work for Massey-Harris, the producer of agricultural machinery. The experience was disappointing: after the high-speed, fully automatic woodcutting machinery I had experienced in my first job, agricultural machinery was crude, uninteresting and uninspiring for learning design. I decided to seek a job in machine-tool fabrication, but the developments of the war changed all my plans.

In April, 1940, Hitler invaded Denmark and Norway under the excuse that he needed their coastline to break the British blockade of Central Europe. The strategic-military aspects of these invasions were far-reaching, but one political feature was most upsetting; local Nazi parties had been organized for years by the Germans; members of these parties were in all walks of life, including the military establishment, and they now sided with the invaders and facilitated the takeover of their country. In Norway, this group was led by a man named Quisling, whose name became synonymous with traitor.

On May 10, 1940, Hitler invaded Holland and Belgium in order to invade France by bypassing the heavily defended German-French frontier. The main features of that invasion included: massive bombing of certain cities, including Rotterdam in Holland to assert German might, motorized troops, which rapidly swarmed through the country, the dive-bombers which dealt with fortified positions, and again, the use of local Nazi parties which betrayed their country.

Within a few weeks, the Germans took Paris, and a new French government under Petain and Laval surrendered to Hitler.

The British and Canadian armies, which had been spread out along the Belgium-French frontier, had to withdraw to the coast, and they were rescued, largely from the port of Dunkirk, by a heroic effort of the British Navy and a lot of small, private, civilian boats.

During these disastrous events, Lloyd George, who had been the Liberal Prime Minister of Great Britain during World War I, got up from his death bed and insisted in Parliament that Chamberlain resign as Prime Minister and that the Conservative maverick, Winston Churchill, who since 1936 had made strong speeches against Hitler, become the head of the British government. Churchill proceeded to form a coalition government, including the Labor Party, offering the country "nothing but blood, sweat and tears".

The British Commonwealth of Nations now "stood alone." The Russians had their pact with Germany. The USA was isolationist and wanted no part of European wars, but the members of the Commonwealth, Canada, Australia, New Zealand and even South Africa, stood by the Crown, actively mobilizing and sending their armies to Great Britain or the Middle East. India, too, was a source of superb soldiers (Sikhs), in spite of what had gone before and what was to happen after the war.

The mood in Great Britain was defiant: in spite of massive air raids on London, which soon commenced, the vast majority of people had no intention to surrender to the Germans, whom they despised, let alone surrendering to that Charley Chaplin-like figure, Adolph Hitler. All talk, that the war is being fought for the Jews, which we had heard occasionally before, ceased in Great Britain. This *was* "their finest hour".

Churchill claimed that a threat of invasion of the British Isles had always existed, even during World War I, and that now there was a greater concentration of British and Canadian armies in the country than ever before. Furthermore, the new Spitfire and Hurricane fighters had assured air supremacy over Dunkirk during the evacuation, boding well for the future, and the British Navy had hardly been affected by the fight in Western Europe.

When the new French government tried to surrender the French fleet to the Germans, the British Navy successfully attacked and destroyed the French fleet at Oran, proving that "they meant business".

## Internment

The German invasion of Holland, Belgium and France brought another wave of Jewish and political refugees to England, but the multitude of disguises that the Germans had used to infiltrate their agents into critical positions made the British population highly suspicious of all foreigners. Severe restrictions and eventual internment were inevitable.

The police came around to my house and told me to sell my bicycle. I could still go to work by bus, but there was little else I could do in the evenings. I fitted all my dire necessities into one big suitcase, ready for internment. The rest of my belongings I stored in the basement of the Steinarts' house.

Soon thereafter, the police left word that I should stay home the next day, and the following day they fetched me in a small police car and took me to Bury, about 12 miles north of Manchester, where an old, disused textile mill had been converted into an internment camp housing about 2000 inmates ranging from loyal-to-Hitler, German Merchant Marine sailors who had been captured by the British Navy, to ultra-Orthodox, Chasidic Jews and German Jesuit priests who had been persecuted remorselessly by the Nazis. The Jesuits aggressively preached all the pacifism and equality of all human beings, which the Catholic hierarchy was too frightened or too uncaring to advance.

For us Orthodox Jews, food became a major problem. There was no kosher meat; the Chassidim believed that even the bread was possibly tainted by having been baked with non-kosher fat. We existed on vegetables and canned fish, like sardines. All food was cooked in coal-fired vats, which, incidentally, made incredibly good coffee, of which we had plenty, since the British population did not drink coffee in those days. At least there never was a lack of a Minyan for morning, afternoon and evening services.

We slept on the floor, on mattresses filled with straw in the big, empty halls of the disused textile factory. Gradually, we cleaned the floor and walls, and our surroundings became more civilized.

There was no lack of interesting people to talk to. An Austrian, socialist, charismatic politician delivered some excellent speeches, demonstrating the compliance of the German upper class allowing the rise of Hitler, and predicting that our internment would not last very long. The Chasidim gave some lectures on Jewish law subjects, but I found their approach shallow. The Nazi German sailors, who expected a successful German invasion any day, assured us that anti-Jewish attitudes would cease now that Germany had enough "lebensraum".

The roof of the old buildings leaked when it rained. Luckily, this was an atypical English summer; there was very little rain.

After about three weeks, we were transferred to a large tent camp, Prees-Heath, near Shrewsbury. Now we, the Orthodox, had our separate group of tents and our own kitchen. Lectures, discussions, an orchestra, cabaret-like performances and physical exercises were organized to fill our day, though the lack of really nourishing food made me feel weaker by the day.

Our lot improved a little bit when we were visited by the son-in-law of the Chief Rabbi of Great Britain, who implored us "not to feel bitter about the British people for this act of panic." He was optimistic that we would be set free pretty soon.

The young assistant of Pastor Niemoeller was one of our fellow internees. Niemoeller was an outspoken anti-Nazi who, from his pulpit in Berlin, never hesitated to criticize the ideology and the misdeeds of the Nazis. He had been a U-boat captain in World War I and therefore was "untouchable"; his removal would have caused a riot in Germany. The same immunity did not extend to his young assistant, who had to flee. We benefited from some interesting lectures on the New Testament given by this young man, who was quite critical of some of the speeches given by our fellow internee Rabbis.

Another unforgettable character from this sojourn in tents was Heini Preiss. He had been in charge of a group of orthodox, German Jewish agricultural trainees, who had been set up on a farm outside Manchester by the German Jewish Aid Committee, pending their immigration to Israel. I had met Preiss on a visit to that farm and realized that he was absolutely brilliant and had an in-depth Jewish education. Now in our tent life I had a chance to listen to Preiss. He never gave a speech or lecture, but was brilliant in discussions. He, too, was very critical of some of the points of views put forward by our Rabbis. By design and by accident, I ran into Preiss several times during the next six years. He gave up

Orthodoxy and became very critical of Zionism, but eventually joined the Jewish Brigade.

My cousin, Hansfried Gans, turned up in the tent camp, together with other internees from the London area. He had claimed Dutch citizenship since our fathers had reverted to our grandfathers' nationality. Eventually, the Dutch Air Force in exile got him out of the internment and he became a flight navigator participating in numerous, adventurous bombing runs over Western Europe and Germany.

As the weather became more inclement in August/September, we were transferred to the Isle of Man, where each internment camp consisted of several blocks of houses that had been boarding houses before the war. Again, we, the Orthodox, had our own houses, right on the "boardwalk", with an extensive barbed wire fence separating us from the sea.

Life was very organized: courses and lectures on a wide variety of subjects were available; I registered for mathematics and mechanical design and got my first exposure to psychology, an analysis of current design of cars and Talmudic Studies.

Rabbi Spitzer, Jr. lived in our house. His father had been the Rabbi of Hamburg. It was generally agreed that the son was a considerably more brilliant Talmudic scholar than the father, but when the son had reached a pinnacle of scholarship, he decided to give up being a Rabbi and study law in a German university. We got the full benefit of his lectures and his application of the Jewish law to current problems.

We did get British newspapers in the camp, and we were keenly aware of the military and political developments that summer: the Germans had to cease raiding Great Britain by day because of excessive losses. In the absence of daylight air supremacy, an invasion was highly unlikely. The USA sold 50 destroyers to the British. This "deal" had to be "sold" to the isolationist Congress by Roosevelt's aids, who pointed out that Roosevelt, who had been the Under Secretary for the Navy in WWI, was a navy "nut", who insisted on the U. S. Navy being equipped with only the latest models of destroyers. We all hoped that this deal was the first indication of the availability of the U. S. industrial power to Great Britain. Chamberlain had to resign from the Cabinet due to ill health. One of my friends, a non-Jewish, German communist then remarked vehemently, "But he (Churchill) must get rid of (Lord) Halifax!" (Later it turned out that Halifax had been negotiating with Hitler behind Churchill's back. How did my friend know?)

In the fall of 1940, the British government lowered from 21 to 18 the age at which "enemy aliens" could join the army. Shortly thereafter, a

Jewish major and his staff came to our camp and after a stormy meeting at which we protested that we would rather join the army as free men, I and a number of other people signed up. I was 18 years old.

## The Pioneer Corps

At the beginning of December, I joined a group of about 15 "volunteers" under the guidance of a corporal, taking the ferryboat back to Liverpool and traveling all night by train to Ilfracombe in Devon, headquarter of those companies of the Pioneer Corps which were made up of aliens.

My two years in the Pioneer Corps were undoubtedly the most frustrating time of my life: I did not have the feeling that I was contributing much to the war effort, and in spite of all the manual labor we were doing on construction projects, I did not learn new skills for my future professional career.

In Ilfracombe we learned the basics for being a soldier: how to wear and polish the uniforms, parade ground drills, mounting guards, getting a multitude of inoculations, and using gas masks, which at that time we had to carry all the time. In the event of an invasion, Hitler was expected to use poison gas. Only later, when Allied bombers dominated the skies over Germany, was the need for carrying gas masks in Britain relaxed.

After three weeks of such activities, a new company was formed and we were sent to Catterick camp, a longtime army base in Yorkshire.

The company was commanded by a major; all our officers were British, colorless, not too bright, and they were far removed from us. Most of them had been officers in WWI. It took almost two years before "enemy aliens" attained the rank of officers in the Pioneer Corps.

Almost all the warrant officers (sergeants) were professional soldiers. They were old and borderline alcoholics, but soon some of our own people were promoted to the rank of sergeant. I was not at all interested in that sort of a career: I wanted to get out, into a fighting unit, and I voiced that desire any time I had an opportunity to talk to visiting authorities. In the British Army, colonels or generals follow their inspection of the paraded troops by inviting complaints. That gave me my chance to point out to higher authority that I was wasting my time doing manual labor while I really wanted to be in a fighting unit.

Once, the company bulletin board published a request for volunteers to become air force pilots. Those were the days when Great Britain, being alone in the war against Hitler, hoped to win the war by totally destroying all German towns. As usual, I volunteered. I was sent to a two-day examination, which I passed with flying colors, and I was assured that I would hear from the air force within a few weeks, but eventually the word came down that the Royal Air Force could not expect its aircrews to share their dangerous mission with an "enemy alien".

For most of us, being in the Pioneer Corps was a depressing and humiliating experience. Our intellectual powers, our education, the skills we had learned, our dedication to the cause of ridding Europe of the Nazi monstrosity were not being utilized; by and large we performed unskilled manual labor in a corps which originally had been created for soldiers who were physically unfit or had a criminal record.

Work was never set out by our own officers, but we were directed by small detachments from the Royal Engineers, or the Army Service Corps or the project managers of civilian contractors. Physical labor was our only contribution, but many of our fellow pioneers had never previously done hard physical work.

Nevertheless, for me there were a lot of interesting new experiences. Some of my colleagues were high-powered intellectuals who loved to talk about their field of specialization. Charley Leyser, who had "read" history at Oxford, was a stimulating guide in discussions even while we were performing our pick and shovel work. These were the days when the Penguin books first appeared; they could be carried (and hidden) easily in the square pockets of our uniforms. "A book a day" became our motto; it certainly allowed me to broaden my knowledge into fields, for which, in a career-driven life, I would not have allowed time. I booked a correspondence course in applied mathematics, but found that I could concentrate on it only on weekends or when I was on leave. Sex was a continuous subject of discussion; all the Austrians were "experts" because they had all studied under Freud. At least that is what they claimed. I openly admitted my lack of knowledge. Similarly, many claimed to have won outstanding titles in track and field sport events.

Some of our fellow Pioneers had been in the French Foreign Legion. They were part of a British-French Expeditionary Force that was sent to the northern tip of Norway when the Germans invaded Norway in 1940, but the Force could not hold its own and was evacuated to England. Some of the ex-legionnaires had interesting histories; others were unsavory characters who had to be kept in line by bribes.

Social life for the class of people to which we now belonged was centered on the pubs (inns), dances organized by charity organizations and canteens (tea and coffee shops set up for servicemen and servicewomen). The pubs did not attract me, since I did not like to waste my money on beer or drinks. The canteens were a pretty dull necessity when there was no alternative way to sit at a table. The dances were a wonderful way of meeting girls, since in Great Britain men and women came to these gatherings without a date. Even highly respectable girls would not hesitate to dance with complete strangers. I had to learn ballroom dancing, but once I had picked up the rudimentary steps, I befriended some very worthwhile young ladies.

Going to the movies at least once a week also became a new experience for me in the Pioneer Corps; in our hometown in Germany the local cinema had displayed a large sign, "Jews Not Desired". While I lived in London and in Manchester, I had neither the time nor the money to see movies regularly.

There were two pleasant surprises for me in army life: we were paid a regular salary and we got seven days of leave once every three months. Since I did not drink or smoke, I now had more pocket money than ever before. For our leaves we got railway tickets to anywhere we wanted to go. On my first leave I went to London for a few days to look at the extensive bomb damage, experience some air raids at night and watch life in the subways, where people took shelter at night. After that, I spent a few days with the Wislickis in Manchester.

On subsequent leaves, I visited my brother Theo, whose boarding school had moved from

Kent, continuously subjected to over-flights of German bombers, to more peaceful Shropshire in the middle of England.

**Private M. Gans in the Pioneer Corp (1941).**

# Yorkshire

We stayed in the huge military base, Catterick Camp in Yorkshire, only for a week or two before being moved to Sedbergh in the Lake District, where we converted a huge estate into a gasoline storage dump. Sedbergh is the home of a famous Public (that means private) school. We had almost no contact with these upper-class, well educated boys, but admired the tough cross country runs to which they would subject themselves. After I had befriended a lovely young lady who was the daughter of the only lawyer in that town, I did get invited to the homes of some of the very interesting teachers of the Public school.

While in Sedbergh I hitchhiked one Sunday afternoon to York, the county seat, to visit my father's cousin, Jack Gans and his wife, Annie. I had heard about them, never had been in touch with them and I came unannounced, but my luck held; they were home.

Jack came from the Dutch part of the family. In the twenties, he had bought a patent in Italy that enabled the conversion of the milk wastes from the manufacture of chocolate products into a plastic. Since Bakalite was the only plastic in large scale use at that time, Jack called his plastic Gansolite. Chemically it was probably similar to nylon, which had not been invented yet. Jack had made an agreement with the Rowntree family in York that he would get all the milk wastes from their chocolate production, converting the wastes into Gansolite, largely used for the manufacture of buttons. By now he and his wife owned a large factory, Jack was the patrician businessman, while Annie, who had been a German opera singer, administered the factory. They were part of high society in York.

Their home was a beautiful estate almost in downtown York, exquisitely furnished. They had no children, but eventually their home became the rallying point for all the Gans family soldiers and airmen of the Free Dutch, American and British armed forces when they passed through England. A few month later, I spent a few days of one of my leaves with them and I got a thorough look at their factory, where they employed several hundred workers, mainly women, who were mobilized for the war effort. My cousin Hansfried, who was a navigator in the Free Dutch Air Force, was with me there at the same time.

**Visit to the house of my father's cousins Annie and Jack Gans in York. From Left to Right: Hansfried Gans (navigator in the Free Dutch Airforce), Annie Gans, and I**

# June 1941

In the spring of 1941, we moved from Sedbergh to an estate south of Edinburgh in Scotland. We used the "park" of that estate to install an ammunition dump. We were housed in the "manor" of the estate, which had been emptied of all its furniture. There were parquet floors in all rooms, into which about 90 of us crowded, sleeping on palliasses (straw filled mattresses). A large room, which probably was the combined dining/ sitting room and atrium of the manor, was our common room for meals, meetings and listening to the radio. There, on Sunday, June 22nd, 1941, while having breakfast, we heard the BBC announcement that Hitler had invaded Russia. We, the younger members of this Pioneer Company, greatly welcomed this momentous event: we just could not see how the British Empire alone could win a war against Hitler, and we felt very strongly that in Munich, in 1938, Britain and France should have insisted on bringing in Russia while negotiating the fate of Czechoslovakia.

On the way to work (we always worked both Saturday and Sunday mornings) we started singing and whistling the "International", much to the annoyance of most of the older members of the company, who were right wing conservatives and cursed us. "If you people were not so stupid, life would be easier for all of us." These were the same people who loudly disapproved of my Jewish orthodoxy; I still laid Tefillin (Phylacteries) every morning and tried to avoid eating meat.

In the evening, we assembled in our spacious dining/common room to listen to Churchill, who, in his inspiring way, clearly set out the direction into which the war effort would be taken now. He said;

"No one has been a more consistent opponent of Communism than I......I will unsay no word that I have spoken about it. But all this fades away before the spectacle which is now unfolding........I see the Russian soldiers standing on the threshold of their native land guarding the fields their fathers have tilled from time immemorial......I see advancing upon all this in hideous onslaught the Nazi war machine......

I have to declare the decision of His Majesty's Government.....any man or state who fights on against Nazidom will have our aid.....

It is not for me to speak of the action of the United States, but if Hitler imagines that his attack on Soviet Russia will cause the slightest divergence of aims..... in the great democracies...      he      is      woefully mistaken.......The Russian danger is, therefore, our danger and the danger of the United States, just as the cause of any Russian fighting for his hearth and home is the cause of free men....in every quarter of the globe....."

We spent the next few months in various locations of the Edinburgh area pouring concrete, building Nissen huts, digging trenches for water pipes, and laying the foundation of roads inside military depots and camps. Usually, we were sufficiently far away from Edinburgh that it paid to go to town only on weekend afternoons. Twice, I attended performances of the d'Oyle Cart Opera Company in the Edinburgh opera house.

For a few weeks we were attached to the first "mixed" (women and men) anti-aircraft battery of the British Army. Those women were intelligent, well educated, self-confident and had the very fast mental and physical reaction essential for anti-aircraft gunners.

Dumfries, in the south of Scotland, was another work station for a few weeks. Once more, we were building storage facilities in the park of a big estate. There, we were given the luxury of a six-foot, motorized concrete mixer; everywhere else we mixed concrete by hand. I volunteered to look after the mixer; compared to the machinery I was used to from my apprenticeship in

Manchester, the mixer was a simple piece of equipment. When it needed repair, I usually devoted my evenings to it as it was summer, and light until 10 o'clock. Repeatedly, I rented a horse from a riding stable in town to keep up the skills I had learned on my uncle's agricultural training farm, and to explore the beautiful landscape. Several of the married fellow Pioneers brought their wives to Dumfries, allowing them to live outside our billets.

In the fall of 1941, we moved to Muirhead, near Glasgow, to build a huge military storage facility. We were billeted in the homes of the civilian population; I had a room to myself, a fellow Pioneer by the name of Ruediger von Etzdorf was assigned to another room in the same home. Ruediger was about two years older than I. We became friends only slowly, but apart from talking late into the night, we did not associate with each other very much. There was a small group of our fellow Pioneers who did not have to live on army pay; they frequented hotels and fancy restaurants, and Ruediger was part of that group. The aristocratic von Etzdorf family had been mildly-anti Nazi. Ruediger had been sent to the Outward Bound school and went with that school to England when its partially Jewish staff, a considerable number of Jewish students, and the cosmopolitan ideals it taught clashed with the Nazi ideology.

Ruediger and I had one common aim: get out of the Pioneer Corp. We schemed until late into the nights how to achieve this aim. Eventually, one of his contacts got him into the Intelligence Section of No. 1 Commando, a few months before the Inter Allied Commando was created. He disappeared from our Pioneer Corp Company and nobody but I knew where he had gone.

(Footnote: In 1943, the Count von Etzdorf, Ruediger's father, traveled with 15 suitcases from Germany to Argentina, There he "changed coats" and traveled with his 15 suitcases to England. Turns out he had been a "double agent" all the time. After the war, I read an article in the Manchester Guardian protesting against the appointment of a von Etzdorf, Ruediger's uncle, to the post of Foreign Secretary in the Adenauer government.)

Glasgow offered the Scottish Symphony Orchestra, whose concerts I attended regularly. Some of us became regular guests of the International Student House, which gave us a chance to attend lectures, discussions and meet some educated girls. Most important to me, a professor of mathematics made himself available once or twice a week to help, free of charge, those, like me, who were taking correspondence mathematics courses.

I befriended an attractive Austrian Jewish girl, who was studying medicine. She was engaged to a young German Jewish man, who was studying Engineering in London. She took me to her home a few times. Her father who was a pretty sharp businessman, never failed to point out, "When you get out of this (the army) at the end of the war, you will be a nobody." That was a very common attitude of people of our own background, who thought that we were fools wasting our time in the army.

## December 1941

We could freely listen to German broadcasts. In Muirhead, the family in whose home we were billeted had a good radio set in their kitchen and they let us use it. At the beginning of December, 1941, the Germans claimed that they were about to occupy Moscow and Leningrad and that the war against Russia was essentially ended. We didn't believe a word of it, but the Japanese must have felt that it was time to join their victorious ally, and in one day they launched a major attack against the U. S. Fleet at Pearl Harbor and a British battleship and aircraft carrier in the Pacific. Our first thoughts were that the overwhelming production capacity of the U. S. would now come into full play.

Three weeks later, Churchill was in Washington. We came back from work just as he started to address the combined session of the U.

S. Congress with one of the greatest speeches ever. "Can it be that they (the Japanese) do not realize that we shall never fail to persevere against them, until we have taught them a lesson which neither they nor the world will ever forget?"

In the spring of 1942, I operated a super-heavy pneumatic drill to break up old concrete slabs, which we then used as a foundation for building roads inside the military storage facility that we were still building near Muirhead. The work exhausted me badly and I came down with hepatitis. I spent a week in the military wing of a nearby hospital and then spent another, very pleasant week in a "mixed" military recuperation home on the Scottish west coast.

## The 440

Also in the spring of 1942, our Pioneer Corp Company was taken over by a more imaginative major. Since our own officers had no influence on the work we did, this major set out to instill some espirit de corp by organizing lectures, cabarets and theater plays in the evenings. He also insisted that we start some competitive sports activities. A 440-yards (¼ mile) race on a very rough track was laid on for one Sunday afternoon. I was only too keen to participate: I had not done any competitive sports since I was 11 years old. When the Nazis came to power, we were barred from sports meetings; "they" could not bear the thought that a Jew might beat an Aryan. But I always loved to run and I had taught myself running techniques from books.

As soon as the race got underway, I realized that of the 30 or so "experts," half of them started running too slow and the other half had started too fast, at a pace they could not maintain. When I came around the last bend there was only one runner ahead of me and I overtook him easily.

I was deliriously happy, but I did not show it: so all these experts who had claimed to have won all these medals in sports, they were just a bunch of phonies; none of them could beat me at any distance. I had put myself "on the map". As I walked back to my billet in Muirhead, I knew that if I would ever write an autobiography, the first chapter would be entitled "I won the 440."

Now we were booked for sports meetings almost every weekend. I usually ran the anchor in a relay; we were rarely beaten. I also ran in cross country competitions, where I was never beaten.

## The End of Marking Time

In the fall of 1942, we spent some more time near Edinburgh. By now, we had two officers of German/Austrian Jewish background. One of them was young; he had just completed a degree in mechanical engineering. I became quite friendly with him. I could not see why he was wasting his time in the Pioneer Corps, but I appreciated that he walked with me to an Edinburgh synagogue on Yom Kippur.

Later in the fall, we went back to the Glasgow area, where we were stationed in Paisley, building a camp for the Americans, who were now coming over in ever-increasing numbers.

Paisley was part of the Glasgow harbor; in those days still more "slummy" than Glasgow.

When the call came to be interviewed for something "special," I was very happy, sure that "special" would represent an elite troop, and I had no doubt that I would be accepted. Five years of being treated as a pariah and four years as a tolerated refugee had come to an end; the dawn of self-emancipation, of a career free of prejudice rose in the early hours on a spring Sunday morning in 1943, over picturesque Aberdovey in North Wales, the training base of 3 Troop, 10 Commando. Within an hour of arrival, I had changed not only my name, but also my identity from Manfred Gans to Fred Gray.

We were urged to have just one "cover address", friends or family, to where mail from our "previous life" could be sent. I chose the Wislickis in Manchester. They were both doctors, were used to being discreet, and they had no children. We had to send to that address any private possessions which could identify our previous life. For me, that meant getting rid of my diary, clothing into which my name had been stitched and, above all, Tallith and Tefillin. I had been "laying" Tefillin every weekday morning since I was 13 years old, even in the Pioneer Corps.

My change of identity was complete. I was keen to accept new challenges.

# X TROOP

## WWII German-Speaking, Parachute Commando Troop of the British Army.

Three Troop of Ten Interallied (IA) Commando had been organized by Lord Mountbatten, the Head of the British "Combined Operations", with the special approval of Prime Minister Winston Churchill, who coined the name X (for unknown) Troop, but that name had to be dropped because it looked too suspicious.

The Troop had 87 members, 19 of whom eventually were killed on battle missions. One was killed in training. Speaking German without a foreign accent was the essential qualification for joining the Troop.

Battlefield interrogations, infiltration into German lines, and long distance patrols were the proposed major tasks of the Troop. In fact, there was at least one of us in every Commando action against the German war machine after 1942, including the sinking of the boat which carried the Heavy Water for Hitler's planned atomic bomb.

Who was in the troop? By Hitler's definition, 90 % of us were Jewish; by Halachic (Jewish Law) definition, approx. 70% were Jewish. Members were from Germany, Austria, Czechoslovakia (2) and Hungary(4). At least four of the members had been politically active (Communist, Socialist, Anti Fascist). I doubt that anyone, apart from myself, was interested in specific Jewish causes. The main motivation for joining was to regain self-respect; we had gone through many years in Germany and Austria being treated like outcasts, pariahs, a race of criminals, racially one step lower than the Kushim (Blacks). In Great Britain, we first were "foreign refugees", then we became enemy aliens, then we were interned and spent 5 months behind barbed wire. Then we were allowed to join the army in an unarmed labor unit in which the British contingent consisted of criminals and physically unfit people. No inducement for anyone to look up to you on the street. No way to be able to befriend girls.

In Aberdovey, the town in Wales where the Troop was first assembled, we were reborn: we now were in the uniform of the elite of the elites.

We had arrived in that very picturesque town in small groups, usually in the very early hours of a Sunday morning. We were taken to a lovely villa up on a hill and there, within an hour or two, we adopted new names, a false history, were given Commando insignias for our uniforms and green berets. We were taken to private homes, where we were "billeted" and there had to play our new identity without slipping up, ever. We were reborn.

Thus started months of incredibly intensive military training, comprising almost daily use of the most modern weapons with live ammunition, being shot at with live ammunition, handling explosives for demolition, exhaustive physical feats, swimming through ocean surfs or rivers in full uniform with weapons, mountaineering, cliff climbing, parachuting, in-depth intelligence classroom work in map reading, German Army organization, German Army weaponry, and wearisome concentration on performing all these activities during the hours of darkness.

We kept in touch with our previous life through a cover address, usually family or close friends. They collected our mail and forwarded it to the assumed name wherever we happened to be. Whenever we were on leave, back to the neighborhoods of our previous life, we had to wear civilian clothing.

This double life led to lots of amusing incidents. I was sent to the Intelligence School in Cambridge University for a week, but my brother was working on a farm near Cambridge and he lived with an orthodox Jewish family in Cambridge. When I wanted to see him in the evening, I had to change into civilian clothing in some toilet, then steal out of the Intelligence School and take a bus to my brother's residence.

We were highly amused to find out that we could legally commit bigamy by getting married under our new name as well as our old name. We relished this life of daring and deception. It was a challenge not to pay for train tickets. We smuggled ourselves onto the trains by some unobtrusive means, then jumped off the train, rolling down the embankment before the train pulled into the station of our destination.

Above all we were superbly fit, and consequently superbly self-confident.

We never fought as a Troop, but there were 1 – 5 of us with every Army Commando or Royal Marine Commando unit which went into action.

**Captain Brian Hilton Jones, the "Skipper"**

**Private F. Gray in Aberdovey 1943**

**My cover address Luise and Leo Wislicki in their garden in Manchester.**

## Intensive Training, Intensive Living and the Beginning of Actions.

Our previous experience in the army – the Pioneer Corp—had been almost a complete waste of time. In contrast, we were now subjected to an intensity of training unique in previous military histories, but now largely imitated by the elite troops of some modern armies. Our environment was organized to allow this intensive training.

We were billeted in private homes, but our hosts had to feed us and clean for us all while putting up with the impossible schedule of our training. They were, of course, reimbursed for that service and they liked to get our ration cards, since our allowance for meat, butter, jams etc were considerably higher than the allowances for civilians. But above all, they wanted to do their bit for the war effort, and they were proud to be helpful to elite soldiers like us.

In Aberdovey, I was billeted with an approximately 50-year-old spinster. She also rented one room to a very nice lady, and that lady's five-year-old daughter, who were evacuees from Birmingham. Between these two ladies, I was well looked after.

Captain Hilton Jones, the "Skipper" of our troop, the mystery man who had interviewed and personally chosen each of us in London, was superbly fit and it was his outspoken aim to get us to the same level of physical conditioning. There were runs along roads, runs up and down the open hills around Aberdovey, speed marches (100 yards running, 100 yards marching) with full equipment, cross country, following maps which mainly showed the contour lines. On one of those marches, we covered 40 miles in one night.

We used our pistols, rifles, Tommy guns, machine guns and mortars almost daily on a range, learned to use the standard British hand grenade, which looks like a lemon and breaks into distinct splinters when it explodes. Whoever throws it has to make sure that he is in "cover" by the time the grenade explodes. The other hand grenade we used was in a plastic container and it contained liquid phosphorous to cause a fire. Again, we had to make sure that after throwing it we were under "cover" by the time the grenade exploded, to avoid being splashed by the phosphorous. We learned how to use explosives, particularly the Bangalore Torpedo, which could be used to blow a path through a minefield.

We used military maps intensively and got lectures on the organization and equipment of the German army.

The physical demands of all these activities never bothered me. All the running competitions I had attended during the last few months in my previous unit had left me super fit. Occasionally, running or marching in the heavy and hard army boots afflicted me with some bad blisters on my feet. Those we cured by cutting the blister open and treating it repeatedly with "rubbing alcohol", a painful procedure, but it ensured that the blister was dried out the following day.

When we were off-duty in the evening, there was little to do. There was no attractive "Pub", no "Tearoom", no movie house, and the public dances, the best way to meet girls in Great Britain, were held only once a month. I attended two of these dances, picked up a very worthwhile girl at each of them, and then had to play my changed identity to the fullest when dating these young ladies.

This lack of social life in Aberdovey was a blessing in disguise; it allowed us to get used to our new identity slowly. Even when we were amongst ourselves, we rarely talked about our previous lives; the less we knew about each other, the less likely we would betray each other if we were taken prisoner on a raid.

## Mountaineering

Captain Hilton Jones, the Skipper, was a native Welshman from a well-to-do family. He had been a student at the University of Cambridge and had an extraordinary talent for languages. By the time he took charge of our troop, he spoke German fluently with hardly any foreign accent (After the war he was in charge of the Swiss offices of the British chemical company I.C.I, and there he learned to speak Switzer Duitsch. When he was put in charge of I.C.I Spain, he became fluent in Spanish). He claimed that he had climbed the mountains and the cliffs of Snowdon already as a young boy. He believed that it was essential that we learn the techniques of cliff climbing (and descending) to improve the versatility of our tactical use. Thus, he took us for a week to the Snowdon mountain region.

We were temporarily billeted in and around the town of Bethesda which is about an hours drive from Aberdovey I shared a tiny room in a tiny house with Colin Anson. (Ascher) Our landlady was about 25 years old, quite good-looking, and she had two children. Her husband was in the Merchant Marines. She was too modest to probe into our true identity, but one day she said to me, "I am not really British either; my father is Jewish."

I just said, "Oh, that sounds interesting."

Every morning, we were taken by truck to the Ydwal Slabs; a row of solid stone bolders, at least 20 feet high. These rocks were ideal to teach us the basic techniques of climbing: look for tiny protrusions for handholds and footholds; keep your body away from the rock - after all, you don't climb stairs by lying on them and pulling yourself up on the banister.

We were taught how to use a rope so that it is always safely on your body, irrespective whether, in a team of three, you have the lead, the middle or the end position. There were techniques for "letting out" the rope when the person ahead of you is climbing, and "hauling in" the rope when the person behind you is climbing.

In these elementary mountaineering lessons on the slabs, we were always on a rope secured by one man sitting on top of the slab. Nevertheless, most of us went through some harrowing moments when we felt we were losing our foot or hand-holds, or could not see a suitable hold to continue the climb.

Soon, we split up in groups of three to tackle the real climbing trails. It took a team of three from two to four hours to safely go from the bottom of a trail to the top. Every day, we climbed one or two different trails. Though all these trails ran more or less parallel to each other, we rarely saw the other teams. There was an ambiance of loneliness when climbing these tough trails.

One day when climbing, we heard the team on the trail next to us shout: "We've had an accident, we need help." We could not see them, they were only 50 yards away, but there was no way for us to reach them by going across the face of the mountain. We continued our climb to the top and then went down on the easiest trail of the mountain, which, luckily, was nearby. There, we met the team, whose lead man, Ernest Lawrence (Lenel) had been injured. They somehow got themselves onto this easy trail.

Lawrence was a very tough, well-educated young man from a well-to-do German Jewish family. He had two faults: he was impatient and had such extreme left-wing views that he despised all officers. On this climb, when unable to find a foothold, he tried to jump a gap, but he did not make it. Luckily, his number two man was George Saunders (Saloschin), the fittest, fastest, most self-confident, most agile member of the troop. When George noticed that Lawrence was falling, he secured his foothold, leaned against the mountain face and hauled in the rope. Lawrence fell past George, but when the rope tightened, George was able to absorb the shock. All this took place within two or three seconds.

When the fall was broken, Lawrence was suspended in mid-air with a bleeding head injury and a concussion. The third man of the team climbed up to a ledge near George, and together they pulled Lawrence up to that ledge and got him over to the easy trail, where we met them. One of our sergeants then went down to the hostel near the Ydwal Slabs and telephoned for a doctor and a mountain stretcher. We knew that to move a person with a concussion, we should get a doctor's permission where possible.

On that day, neither the Skipper nor any of our other officers were with us. It took about an hour or two before the doctor and the stretcher came up. By that time, Lawrence was fully conscious and we had bandaged up his wound. The doctor told us to transfer him to the mountain stretcher, which has two oversized skis where normal stretchers have legs. A rope, which is led out slowly, holds the stretcher at the head end of the injured, and another rope at the foot end is used by the guide of the stretcher who, while walking down the trail, keeps the stretcher on or near the trail.

We were just about ready to set all this into motion when a man came walking across the face of the mountain, that means at a 90 degree angle to all the trails, as if he was walking on air. He was in civilian clothing, and after looking at our preparation, he said very firmly, "You are doing this all wrong." We, of–course, were reluctant to take orders from a civilian, but eventually we retied the ropes of the stretcher in accordance with his instructions. He then proceeded to guide the stretcher down the mountain, and since he could walk on air, he chose a path which was smoother than the trail.

As we were letting out the rope to get the stretcher down the mountain, two sergeants from the Mountain Division with large coils of heavy rope across their bodies came down the trail. We asked them, "Who is this man who can walk on air?" To which they replied, "Oh, that is Commander Smyth from the Himalaya expedition." (First expedition to get to the top of Mount Kandel in 1931.)

Two times during our stay in Wales the Skipper made us walk up Mount Snowdon along a narrow path which leads over ridges with steep cliffs on both sides. All this in hauling winds made worse by occasional rainstorms. Frequently, the Skipper was furious that we did not maintain our walking discipline (walk in single file, with a constant distance between persons). But some men were just too afraid to navigate these ridge paths at a fast pace.

We all agreed that mountaineering was mentally and physically the toughest training we had experienced. Climbing up a trail of a cliff can involve several hours of concentrated attention to minute details to avoid a disaster, while pulling, pushing and stretching with every muscle in your body. The occasional stunning views of the valleys, mountains, towns and villages when looking back often only add to the sense of danger.

## Eastbourne

The individual troops of No. 10 Inter-Allied Commando, which had been formed in 1942/43, were initially assembled in different towns along the coast of North Wales. The Commando headquarters were in Harlech. No 1 Troop was French; No 2 Troop was Dutch; we were No 3 (the British) Troop; No 4 was Belgian; No 5 was Norwegian and No. 6 was Polish.

At the end of May 1943, we all moved to Eastbourne, a coastal town in southeast England. Colonel Lister, the commanding officer of 10 IA Commando, an ex-British army boxing champion, hoped to mould all these different nationalities into a more coherent unit. We very much doubted the need for such coherent interaction; it stood to reason that the war actions of each troop would be governed by strategic-political considerations, and we would never fight as a unit. The Norwegians had already been involved in raids on the Norwegian coast and they, as well as all the other Army and Marine Commandos would not undertake a raid without at least one of us, from the German-speaking troop, being present

Again, we were billeted with civilian families, each troop being assigned a section of the town. I shared a room with Andrew Kershaw (Kirchner)

in the house of a young woman who had two children, a boy of 5 years old and a girl of 3 years old. Her husband was in the Royal Air Force in North Africa. The house was about 100 yards away from a municipal town gas tank (that is the mixture of hydrogen and carbon monoxide used for heating and cooking). The tank was guarded by one Bofors quick firing anti-aircraft gun.

By this time, summer 1943, German air raids on Great Britain generally were rare because of the air superiority of the British fighter planes, but raids by single German airplanes on coastal towns like Eastbourne were still quite frequent. Long, wailing air raid alarms were common, particularly at night, but neither we nor the population took much notice of them, except that it alerted us to listen for the "cuckoo", repeated short blasts of the siren, which signified "enemy airplane overhead".

One lovely Sunday morning, Andrew Kershaw and I were having our lunch in our landlady's dining room, when we heard the "cuckoo" and an approaching low flying aircraft. Our landlady hurried her children into the table shelter in their ground-floor bedroom. We rushed outside into the garden and caught a glimpse of a German fighter airplane making a run on the gas tank. Amazingly, the anti-aircraft gun was not firing. The airplane made a sharp turn to the left just before the tank and we could clearly see the pilot in the cockpit, who seemed to be looking at us. We cursed that our Tommy guns were in our upstairs bedroom - too late the raid was over. We rushed outside onto the street to see whether any damage had been done. No sign of damage, not even to the gas tank. The sergeant in charge of the anti-aircraft gun came running along the street towards his gun. In passing, he breathlessly informed us, "We took the bloody gun apart this morning for cleaning."

The intensity of our training continued unabated: speed marches, weapons training, climbing cliffs of dubious integrity, marching straight across country on a compass bearing while adhering to strict time schedules, but there were few combined operations with the other troops of 10IA Commando.

Eastbourne had two big benefits for us: closeness to London, and the efficiency of the southern England electric train service made it very worthwhile to make use of metropolitan amenities such as theaters, concerts and upscale restaurants on weekends. The other benefit of Eastbourne was the dance hall, Wintergarden, which was open every night, where women and men came without a "date", allowing the meeting of girls of many different backgrounds, including young women of the Army, Navy and Air Force Auxiliaries who were stationed nearby. Some of us made a point of going dancing after the most exhausting marches.

Though the attempt to weld the different troops of 10IA Commando with their different nationalities into one coherent fighting unit was not making much progress, it was decided to have an inter-commando cross country race competition. Each troop designated 10 members to represent the Troop. The course was 8-10 miles. There were guides to point the way stationed along the course; we neither knew the direction nor the length of the course.

About 100 yards into the race, George Saunders and I found ourselves at the rear of the pack, though we were regarded as the best runners in 3 Troop. Everybody else had started off in a sprint. In these long races, it is extremely important to use the first few minutes to check your body's posture, arm movements and stride without increasing the rate and depth of breathing. Once we were set, we increased our speed and began to overtake other contestants. We ran through roads and footpaths for several miles until we came to a rather steep hill without a distinct path, truly cross-country. There were still about 15 runners ahead of us when we came to the bottom of the hill, but when we reached the top, we had overtaken everybody except one Belgian sergeant who was tall and had a magnificent stride. He "stuck" with us. We were now back on roads, going through a beautiful part of Eastbourne, and we really "put on the speed", practically sprinting the last two miles

George won the race, the Belgium sergeant was second and I was third. Peter Moody (Kurt Meier), who had really been a running champion in the Maccabi sports club in Germany, came in 4th; Bartlett (Bilman) who had been a musician in the Bavarian Symphony orchestra and who was a little older than most of us, came in 5th. By the time the 13th or 14th contestant had reached the finishing line, all the members of 3 Troop had been accounted for; we had won the race by a huge margin. Our performance in the cross-country race "put us on the map"; it markedly increased the awareness of the other 10 Commando troops of our capabilities.

From the finishing line, at which Colonel Lister himself was taking all the data, I walked back to our headquarters to get my clothes. The Skipper was just leaving. When he saw me, he said, "I hear you did very well". It would be 25 years, when fortuitously, our paths crossed again, before I got another compliment from him.

One glorious summer day - I think it was the Friday before the Bank Holiday - we were taken to Sandhurst, the Officer Training Center of the British Army, to listen to lectures on British Army formations and tactics. In the afternoon, a Tank Corp officer gave us suggestions on how lightly armed troops like us might deal with an enemy tank. We were not convinced that his proposals would work, so the lecture became a polite, but stubborn, discussion.

At the end of this instructive day, at about 5 o'clock in the afternoon, we smartly fell into formation on the hallowed parade ground of Sandhurst. There the Skipper said, "Dismissed. I will see you all tomorrow morning at 9 o'clock on our parade ground in Eastbourne."

Most of us rushed to the nearest railway station with the intention of taking any train that was going east. At the station, we did our usual trick of going into the tea bar, flirting with the girls who were serving there and then waiting for the right moment to get out onto the platform side of the tea bar. The train we eventually caught went through Croydon, the major railway junction point for almost all the trains going south from London. There, we learned that there would be no more trains to Eastbourne that night, but we got on a train to Brighton, which is about 20 miles west of Eastbourne, on the southern coast of England. All these trains were overcrowded, partly because of the upcoming long weekend.

In Brighton, we looked for and found a dance hall at the eastern end of town. It was now 11 o'clock at night and the dancehall would close soon. There were some Canadian units stationed between Brighton and Eastbourne and we were sure that on a Friday night, some of them had come to "town" by truck. There were six of us, and we soon found a group of Canadian signalers who were going into our direction. They took us past their camp, but they had to drop us off about 10 miles from Eastbourne because they didn't want to be caught wasting gas on an unauthorized ride

We covered the remaining 10 miles in two hours. I was starving because we had not had any food since lunchtime. In rationed Great Britain, it was hard to get digestible food "on the fly". As we were speed marching towards Eastbourne, I was craving for the chocolate powder and the heavy oatmeal and raisin cookies our landlady always left for us when we came home late so that we could make a hot chocolate drink. It all worked out fine: by 3 o'clock I was in bed, relaxed and happy. My roommate, Andrew Kershaw, had not made it back. In fact, most members of the troop only returned in the morning just in time for the 9 o'clock roll call on our parade ground.

## Littlehampton

In the middle of September 1943, 3 Troop was assigned to Littlehampton, a coastal town about 40 miles west of Eastbourne. There were a number of bed-and-breakfast hostels near the seafront, and Andrew Kershaw and I were assigned to one of them together with Maurice Latimer (Moritz Levy), Peter Masters (Arany) and Tony Firth (Hans Georg Fuert). By this time, Andrew and I had become good friends and I met his girlfriend, Mary, who stayed with us several times in Eastbourne. Our young landlady in Eastbourne did not mind that we "brought in" girls. To us, Mary was very impressive because she had a law degree from Oxford, while we had barely finished High School, before internment and joining the army. Soon, Andrew got engaged to Mary, and they got married a year later before Andrew went overseas.

Our bed-and-breakfast hostel was run by a middle-aged woman, Miss Thompson, who was also looking after her aged parents. The family lived in the first and second floors, while we had our bedrooms on the third and fourth floor, but we also used the dining room and living room on the first floor. As we moved in, Miss Thompson told us in no uncertain terms that anyone coming home drunk would have to leave and, of course, no girls in the house!

A few days after we arrived in Littlehampton, about a dozen members of our Troop were transferred to Commando units in North Africa preparing to land in Sicily, Italy and Yugoslavia. Most of those who were in this Mediterranean detachment I did not see again until after the end of the war. About the same time, the Skipper, at a meeting in our headquarters, requested that anyone who did not want to be trained as a parachutist should come and see him privately. Only Laddy (Lewinsky) and Webster (Weinberger) made use of this offer. Laddie, who was older than most of us, was a man with a lot of empathy. He married a woman in her late thirties in Aberdovey, and she was now expecting a child. He said, "I have made up my mind that I am going to die on a ship, not in the air." Webster said that he had promised his wife that he would not become a paratrooper. Both of them lost their lives on D-Day, when their landing crafts were hit.

## Ringway

The British training school for parachute jumping was in Ringway, the Manchester airport. While living in Manchester I had visited the airport once by bicycle on a sunny Sunday afternoon.

When we arrived at Ringway, I was struck by the huge hangars that had been added, and which now contained the training and housing facilities of the parachute school. We soon learned that the normal on-the-ground training period for army paratroopers was one to three weeks, but we would be allowed only three days before actually jumping because we were judged to be fit and adaptable.

In those three days, we learned the structure of the parachute, the way it is supposed to unfold guided by the tear strings of different strengths, and the system of belts and locks, which supports the person using the parachute. We visited the clean room-like facilities where, on huge tables, women of the air force auxiliary folded the parachutes under a system of careful checks and supervision.

The British parachutists exited the airplane through a round trap door in the bottom of the fuselage of the 'plane. To make a "clean" exit, we sat next to the trap door, then swung our legs into the opening and then pushed off with our hands with enough force that neither body nor equipment would touch the near end of the trap door, but sufficiently gently to avoid touching the far end of the trap door. After the push off, the hands had to grab the sides of the trousers, with elbows touching the body. This assures going through the slipstream – winds of at least 120 mph – in total symmetry. The least deviation from symmetry would cause spinning of the body and twisting of the parachute into what was called a "Roman candle". All this was extensively practiced from mock fuselages while landing on soft ground covers.

There were similar detailed instructions and exercises on what to do once the chute was developed and, above all, what to do to prepare and execute a soft landing.

The most important apparatus for practicing landings consisted of a 20ft.- high platform from which we could reach a cable with a parachute harness. We would put on the harness and jump off the platform while the instructor would gradually let out the cable through a braking mechanism. Thus, we would swing to and fro several times while going down. Depending on the direction of the swing motion, we had to change the direction of our feet in order to be able to perform the prescribed soft landing on gym mats.

The Skipper, as usual, was the first to try this apparatus, but when he jumped, the braking mechanism failed (or the instructor was not ready) and he landed on the concrete floor, spraining his ankle. Nevertheless, he continued the course and joined us in all the subsequent jumps. The first time I went through this exercise, I had a pretty hard landing and I felt concussed with a fierce headache. The second attempt resulted in a similarly hard landing, but it wiped out the concussion and headache of the first landing. Subsequent jumps were faultless.

I remember that day well because it was Yom Kippur. Of course, I did not fast, but in the evening I took a bus to Manchester and visited my friends, the Wislickis, for the breaking-the-fast meal.

The following day, we were ready for our balloon jump. Five of us at a time were lifted to 700 feet in the gondola of a stationary balloon. Everybody who lived in Great Britain during World War II was very familiar with these balloons; they floated all over towns, their steel cables forcing the German airplanes to stay high up in the sky, preventing below-the-radar sneak attacks.

The gondola, with its large open trapdoor in its floor, looked flimsy and unsafe. When we reached 700 feet, we hooked the extension of our parachute into a sturdy ring, which was part of the cables, and structures that linked the gondola to the balloon. When it was our turn to jump, we sat down next to the trapdoor, swung our legs into the large opening and pushed off.

I knew I had made a good exit. All parts of my harness were in good position, so I looked up and watched the parachute unfold, and then as my fall gathered speed, it opened up to its full diameter, slowing down my descent. An instructor with a megaphone commented on our positioning in the harness as we were approaching ground. My landing was smooth and soft.

During the next few days, we made eight jumps from airplanes

The airplanes used at Ringway were Whitley Armstrongs, whose fuselages were stripped, allowing ten of us (called a "stick") to sit on the floor. Halfway between the crew cabin and the tale end of the airplane was a trap door whose diameter was almost equal to the width of the fuselage. Two "static wires" ran along the roof of the fuselage. We hooked the extension of our parachutes into these wires before sitting down on the floor, five men on either side of the trap door, with our backs leaning on the side of the fuselage. The instructor was in the tail end of the airplane, shouting orders that were so commanding they overcame all our hesitations, practically sweeping us one by one out of the airplane.

When we approached the "target", the instructor, on a signal from the pilot, shouted "open doors", and the first two men of the "stick" who sat on either side of the door then proceeded to open the doors, exposing us to the wind of the slipstream, and possibly a view of the target area.

On the next signal from the pilot, the instructor shouted, "Exit airplane Number One, Number Two......." until everyone was "swept out" by his overpowering commands.

Jumping into the slipstream of an airplane feels like jumping into something solid but pliable; it is less scary than jumping from a balloon, which feels like jumping into "sweet nothing at all". Actually, the slipstream is very dangerous; when the parachute is fully extended and has broken off the static line, it will be swept towards the rear of the airplane, where it will "develop", or open. It will develop so fast that the paratrooper gets the feeling that the parachute is opening on his side, not above him. This is the condition that leads to "thrown lines", where some of the lines of the parachute finish up on top of the canopy, cutting down the area of the parachute. When that condition occurred, we were supposed to pull out our knives and cut the thrown lines.

If the paratrooper's body is in any way asymmetrical, the body will spin and twist the lines into a "Roman Candle", which also prevents the parachute from opening up. To counter the spinning motion, we were supposed to throw ourselves in the opposite direction of the spin. This happened to me once in a later jump and I got myself out of the spin by throwing myself carefully into an opposite spin.

Most of us had never flown in an airplane. Our first jump was our first flight.

After the third jump, while I was rolling up my parachute, another stick from Three Troop was coming down. Looking up, I noticed that Sayers (Sauer), who was about ten years older than most of us, was going to land very close to me. I shouted up to him, "Sayers, f you touch my clean parachute, there will be hell to pay." He landed, groaning and moaning, and after he had collected himself, he turned around to me and said in his Hungarian/ English accent, "Freddie, and I still tell you, it is not the right way to go out of an airplane!"

When we were flying for the fourth jump the pilot could not find the target area, and he had to take us back to Ringway, where we had our first experience of a normal landing. For the sixth jump, the instructor in the airplane gave no more commanding orders. He just said, "Gentlemen, when you are ready, get out," which is psychologically harder to take than sweeping orders.

While we were taking our rush course, several companies from the airborne division were put through the normal physical training and parachute jumping routine. Also, some older men were training to be dropped as spies into Europe. They were trained to be dropped into a lake for a really soft landing.

We witnessed one fatality: a paratrooper whose 'chute was blown against the airplane's rear wheel shield. It turned out that that shield was damaged and the 'chute was ripped apart

At the end of the course, we proudly could put the parachute wings on our uniform. Apart from heightened self-confidence, I took away from the course an important principle of the instructors, who used to preach, "If you feel sorry for yourself, get out of here, you won't jump." It is a principle that applies to many other situations in life.

## Back to Littlehampton

We returned to our billets in Littlehampton, resuming our routine of weapons training, speed marches, night exercises and lectures. As a unit, we rarely did parade ground drills, but I noticed that after our parachute training, we were considerably more cohesive. When we marched through the town as a troop, we were as synchronized as the Guards regiments, a clear indication that parachuting had raised our speed of reaction.

The diversions for our off-duty life in Littlehampton were numerous. London, with its rich life of concerts, theatres, good restaurants and teatime dances to meet more sophisticated girls, was only one hour away by electric train, making it worthwhile going for even just an evening. Then there was a dance hall open almost every evening to meet local girls. But now there was the complication of the American soldiers, whose numbers seemed to increase by the week. They were not used to these "open" dances. When they asked a girl for a dance, they regarded that girl as their "date", and they got very upset when the girl refused that arrangement and continued to dance with other men. Noisy scenes then ensued. Eventually, the dance hall owner had to call the American Military Police.

At one of these dances, I met a group of teenage girls who belonged to a squash club, and they invited me to learn that very fast game. This was long before I learned to play tennis.

The town also had a small cinema, which occasionally showed worthwhile movies. One time, a film entitled "No Margin for Error" was being shown. It was based on the incident in New York, before the USA got into the war, when after a noisy demonstration by Jewish organizations in front of the German Consulate, the Germans reminded Mayor La Guardia that he was responsible for their safety. La Guardia then detailed only Jewish policemen to guard the Consulate. The film, which is based on the interaction of these guards and the German consulate staff, never mentioned that anyone was Jewish, but with policemen with such names as Mo Finkelstein, we knew what it was all about. We also recognized the characters of the German staff, all very funny to us, but the rest of the audience didn't understand it. We laughed so much that Peter Moody said, "We are blowing our security."

In time, we persuaded our landlady, Mrs. Thompson, to allow our fiancées/girlfriends who visited us from out of town for a weekend to stay in a second floor bedroom, provided there were at least two girls "to keep an eye on each other". Our bedrooms were on the third and fourth floor. This arrangement made life a bit easier for us, since we could not get away every week-end. Maurice Latimer, who was dating a Wren (Women Auxiliary of the Royal Navy) who visited us regularly. Maurice married her after the war

## Operation Crossbow

Sometime in the early months of 1944, the Troop was assembled outside the British Legion Hall in Littlehampton for an inspection by Major General Sir Robert G. Sturges, the highest ranking Commando officer we had ever met. After the formal parade and inspection we assembled in the second floor meeting room of the Legion Hall. Extraordinary precautions were taken to assure that nobody could eavesdrop on this meeting. The Major General, who was a small man wearing his green beret straight on his head, then informed us that we had been chosen to get some very special information from an area in Europe that was some distance from the coast. We would work in small groups of three to six people. We would be dropped by parachute near the target area and then make our way back to the coast, where we would be picked up by the Royal Navy. We would get special instruments to observe our target, and there would be at least three methods to get the results of our findings back to Great Britain.

During the following weeks our training became still more intensive as we tried to learn additional skills, or tried to adept learned skills to the specific needs of this new assignment

We were issued newly developed Tommy guns, which were shorter and could be held firmly on the body between the belt and a shoulder strap. Thus, the gun could be carried under the parachute jacket and would not interfere with the harness of the parachute.

We were aware that, for this type of a reconnaissance raid, the airplane that carried us would have to be part of the fleet of Allied bombers which pounded Germany and German military targets in France, Belgium and Holland almost every night. Our airplane would have to be a bomber. We had made one jump from a Halifax bomber in the fall of 1943, and the results had not been good; the plane cannot slow down to less than 230 miles per hour, thus the "stick" of paratroopers is spread out too much. Furthermore, the trap door is near the rear of the plane, it can only be approached from one side, slowing the exit of the "stick" further contributing to spreading the "stick" on the ground.

The target of our raid was to be photographed with an infra-red camera, and the film would then be attached to a carrier pigeon to transport it back to England. That meant that at least one man in each "stick" would jump with a pigeon cage tied to his chest.

Each stick would have at least one newly developed signaling instrument, the S-Phone, to allow talking to an overhead plane and talking to the boats which were supposed to pick us up from the European coast. I was the designated signaler in my stick. The individual parts of the S-Phone were packed in webbing boxes mounted on a belt, which I could wear under the parachute jacket. We had one rendezvous with a Mosquito bomber to try out the S-Phone. The bomber found us easily; it circled overhead for some time, but the telephone never worked.

After completing our reconnaissance mission, we were supposed to return to a stretch of the coast that consisted of steep limestone cliffs, like the white cliffs of Dover. The Germans had not fortified these cliffs and rarely sent a patrol there because no invasion force could have landed at the foot of these steep cliffs. We would wait on top of the cliff until we had made contact with the naval team that would come to meet us. We would then rappel down the cliff on ropes that had been with us since we parachuted from the bomber.

We had learned rappelling as part of the mountaineering course, but it was unthinkable that we could parachute and then "schlep" those heavy ropes for three days. A hemp rope about half the diameter of the standard mountaineering rope was found, and we proceeded to try it for rappelling in the Black Rabbit stone quarry near Littlehampton.

In rappelling, the rope passes between the legs, under one of the legs and then comes up on the back, passing over the opposite shoulder. Enough friction is created by passing of the rope under one of the legs and then up the back and over the shoulder that the additional friction of grabbing the rope with one hand and letting it out with the other hand gives total control over the speed of descent. But with the thinner ropes, we had difficulties slowing down the speed of descent to a comfortable range. The friction between the rope and the upper leg trousers burned a hole into the trousers and would continue to burn the skin of our upper leg.

To overcome this problem, we developed a short belt about three inches wide studded with aluminum squares, which we could wrap around our upper leg for rappelling.

# Dress Rehearsal

For a dress rehearsal of our reconnaissance mission, we were organized into four "sticks" of about 10 people, and each stick was taken by truck to different parts of Sussex in the middle of the night. We were supposed to make our way to the Seven Sisters limestone cliffs in two nights, hiding by day. Neither the local Home Guard nor the military units in the area had been warned of our rehearsal. Having to hide from them made the exercise very realistic.

Sergeant Stewart (David Strauss) was in charge of my stick. Like myself, he was a good map-reader and we decided on a route that would avoid villages and farmhouses, but the massive Canadian and British military camps were not shown on our maps, and we had to avoid them. We moved only at night; during the day we hid and rested in small forests, away from any houses. Once, a farmer with a dog was approaching the woods in which we were hiding, but luckily, they turned off before they reached us.

During the second night of our silent but rapid move towards the coast, we suddenly found ourselves at the entrance of a military camp. (It turned out to be a Canadian camp). The night was pitch dark, rare in open country, and we had great difficulty in identifying the objects ahead.

We were suddenly challenged by a guard, and since we did not answer but tried to retreat, the guard fired on us with a rifle. He didn't hit anybody, since we had taken cover after his first challenge. Stewart realized that we were risking being followed by a well-armed patrol. Very courageously, he exposed himself to the guard, who let him into the camp to give the duty officer an explanation of what we were doing. He came back to us after about half an hour and we proceeded on our way to the coast. Less than eight month later, Sergeant Stewart was given a "Commission in the Field"; that means he became an officer without going to Officer's Training School, and he was put in charge of the whole of Three Troop because by that time, all our officers were either injured or in German prison camps, or both. Stewart was outstandingly intelligent, fit, friendly, courageous and modest.

We reached the coast at the 150-200 foot high Seven Sisters Cliffs at the appointed time, together with all the other "sticks" of Three Troop which had been sent on this realistic rehearsal. After we had confirmed with our S-Phones that ships were waiting for us, we prepared to rappel down the cliffs, every "stick" with its own ropes.

To get these light ropes down without entangling them on protrusions, we had to tie the rope like a harness around the lead man, who then went over the edge of the cliff while two or three men let out the rope slowly. The lead man used his feet to stay away from the face of the cliff. Once the rope stretched from the top to the bottom of the cliff, everybody could rappel down.

While making all these preparations, we learned that the lead man from another stick, Carson (Carlebach), had apparently come off the rope and had taken a very bad fall. It behooved us to be careful, but even without this warning, Stewart would have insisted that we meticulously stick to the rules. We put on the aluminum studded little belts to protect the upper part of our legs and successfully let down our lead man without wasting much time.

I was the second or third person to rappel down. I had not gone very far when I noticed that the rope was not staying on the protective belt. At –first, I decided not to take any notice, but soon the friction generated by the high velocity of my body passing the rope burned through the two pairs of trousers I was wearing, and it was burning my leg. While trying to adjust the belt, the rope came totally off my body. But for my gloved hands holding onto the rope, I was in a free fall down that 150 feet cliff.

For a split second, I saw the gates of another world: the sky lit up to a bright dawn, there was a huge dark red house or stage and huge golden curtains in vigorous motion leading into the house. Then I came back to reality and I had only one thought: make a perfect parachute landing. I held on to the rope as hard as I could. Soon, the rope burnt through the two pairs of gloves I was wearing, and it soon started to burn the skin of all my fingers, but I hit the ground at a spot where there was a soft gravel surface. I made a perfect parachute landing and I walked away without any concussion, bruises or sprains. The burnt fingers and the burn on the upper leg, I soaked in seawater and that stopped the bleeding and the pain. Nobody even noticed that I had been in trouble.

When the whole stick had come down, we collected our packs and weapons that we had let down separately. We then took our turn to wade to the rubber boat operated by one of the Three Troup members who had not agreed to become as parachutist, and we rowed to the "dorey", the silent motorboat which was to take us to an M. T. B. (Motor Torpedo Boat).

Lt. George Lane was in the rubber boat. He said that he did not expect Carson to live until the morning, but he was to be proven wrong. Carson spent several months in hospitals and rehabilitation centers. He did recover, but he had to be invalided out of the army.

A falling stone hit the knee of Hugh Frazer as he was rappelling down the cliff. I had known

Hugh since our early Pioneer Corps time. He, too, was injured badly so that, eventually, he had to be discharged from the army.

The MTB took us to Newhaven. From there, we went by truck back to Littlehampton, where we arrived early in the morning. I went straight to the Army Medical Post, where my burnt fingers and leg were treated and bandaged.

The following day, when we assembled in the lecture room next to our troop headquarters, the Skipper was obviously upset about the rappelling casualties. He implied that we were using too much of our own initiative instead of adhering to tried and tested techniques. He then showed us the latest development in military rappelling procedure: a very thin nylon rope guaranteed to support weights of 300 pounds. While a reel of this rope was being passed around, someone also passed a reel of sewing machine thread, to show our disbelief.

The Skipper never expected us to take any risks that he was not willing to take himself. The following day, he and a school friend, Lieutenant Treffor Matthews, who had only just transferred into Three Troop, went to the Black Rabbit quarry to demonstrate the new nylon rope. The skipper rappelled down the 50 foot wall of the quarry smoothly, but when Lt. Matthews had gone down only a few feet, the nylon rope broke and he fell down to the bottom of the quarry. A protruding ledge broke his fall slightly. Though severely injured, he had no concussion. He spent many months in hospitals and then had to be discharged from the army.

The breaking of the nylon rope was attributed to the fact that the rope, as it was going over the edge of the quarry wall, was rubbing on a sharp rock. It was proposed that, in future, the rope was to be cushioned at the point where it went over the rim of the wall, or cliff. I still had my doubts that all this reasoning was correct. I felt that a 150-pound man whose rappelling movements were not as smooth as the experienced movements of the Skipper could easily generate a dynamic load higher than the 300 pounds static load for which the rope was tested and guaranteed.

Peter Masters proposed the real solution to our problem of needing rappelling ropes to escape from the European coast at a point of sheer cliffs that were hardly guarded by the Germans. Peter suggested that full-size mountaineering ropes be carried by the rubber boat that was supposed to meet us. On making contact by S-Phone, we would lower the nylon rope equipped with a blue signal light to the bottom of the cliff, and we would use the nylon rope only to pull up the real mountaineering rope.

We did not get a chance to try this new procedure. Major-General Sturges visited us again and announced that the information we were supposed to get had been obtained by other means. Other tasks were being prepared for us, but he would not stand in the way of those who wanted to apply to an Officers Training School.

It appeared that many members of the Troop had ambitions to become officers, but the Skipper would recommend only four of them: Dwelly (Goldschmied), Firth (Furt), Kershaw (Kirchner) and Kingsley (Loewenstein). Others, including myself, were not interested in becoming officers: it was obvious that there would be a massive invasion of Europe within a few weeks, and we were not willing to waste four months in an Officers Training School.

Soon thereafter, we realized that in Operation Crossbow, we were supposed to photograph the launching sites of the V1 bombers, the pilot-less bombers which Hitler was about to launch against England.

### Air Sea Rescue.

Social life in Great Britain takes place mainly in the pubs, the often very cozy public drinking places, which, during wartime, served mainly beer and occasionally some substandard food

We had found such a cozy pub near our billet, and a few of us spent time there frequently in the evening. The other regulars were the crew of an Air Sea Rescue boat. They claimed they could develop a speed of 70 miles per hour on the Channel. After we had become friends, they invited three of us to go out with them on a night patrol mission. We readily got permission from the Skipper to accept this invitation.

The air-sea rescue boats went into action every night the Allied bomber fleet was sent out to bomb targets on the European continent. By now, April, 1944, there were massive actions almost every night.

We set out from the Littlehampton harbor, it was more of an inlet than an harbor, one dark, late evening. The regular crew of this boat consisted of two officers, the Captain, the Navigator, and a crew of three sailors. We spent most of our time on the bridge with the Navigator, which allowed us to follow our course on the naval maps. The extent of the German minefields off the coast of France and Belgium, all shown on these maps, really surprised us. We patrolled just outside these minefields.

Unexpectedly, the weather turned really nasty: howling winds and heavy rain. The sea also became very lively, and our ship was thrown around like a rubber ball. We, the non-sailors, became incredibly seasick. It felt as if my stomach was turning inside out. It was impossible to go below deck into the cabin; I had to hold on for dear life on the deck, which got severely sprayed by the wild waves, soaking my clothing in seawater.

By dawn, we were heading back to the coast of England. The Captain announced that in this storm it was not safe to go back to Littlehampton, with its narrow inlet, and that we would try to go to Seaford, which had a harbor behind a seawall. The seawall, also had a narrow entrance through which the ship had to pass without hitting the concrete posts of the wall. The Captain tried to time the passage of the ship to have no interference from the waves, but he was not completely successful, and he had to reverse the direction of the propeller within seconds to avoid being thrown against the posts of the seawall.

Once inside the harbor, all was calm and the boat was berthed quickly. We gathered in the cabin. Our hosts offered us breakfast, but we, the three Commandos, could not even look at food. We were totally exhausted and soaking wet. We wondered how, after a night passage like this, we could possibly have the strength to engage an enemy on the beaches at dawn.

We walked to the railway station and took the train back to Littlehampton.

In the following two or three weeks we went through a lot of exercises with hand grenades and live ammunition, mainly to rehearse street fighting tactics. Two more members of our Troop were injured so severely, that they were unfit to go into action for many months. In one of these incidents, my left hand was sprayed with liquid phosphorous. We were on the other side of the river from Littlehampton. I ran to the river and kept my hand under water until a row boast came along whose crew agreed to take me across the river. I had wrapped my hand in a "fatigue" hat which I had soaked in the river water Once across, I ran a mile or two to the Medical Post for treatment.

The next three days I did not have to participate in any exercise, which suited me fine because I was starved to read some good books prior to having to devote all my time to preparation for the invasion.

## Western Europe including Great Britain and Ireland.

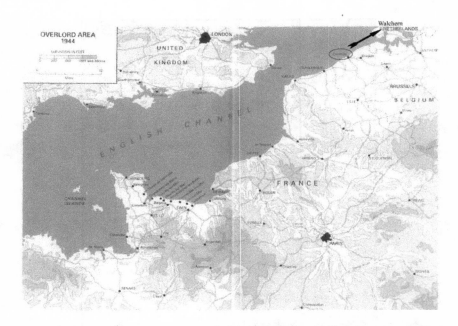

## Map of Western Europe: France, Belgium, Holland, Western Germany, and South of England.

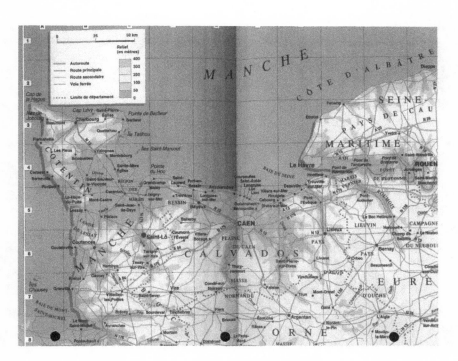

**Map of present day Normandy.**

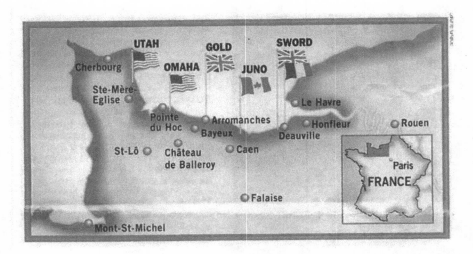

**Landing beaches for the D-Day invasion.**

# D-Day

Beginning of May 1944, 3 Troop 10 I A Commando, the German speaking Troop, temporarily ceased to exist: all the remaining combat-ready members who had not been detailed to Commando units in North Africa, Italy or Yugoslavia were split up amongst those Commando units which were scheduled for the invasion of Northern Europe. There were at least four of us with every Royal Marine or Army Commando unit. (A "Commando" unit consisted of about 450 soldiers, equivalent to one battalion).

Together with 3 Troop's Sgt. Major O'Neill (Oskar Hentschel,Austrian), Maurice Latimer, (Moritz Levy, Czech) and Tommy Swinton (Schwytzer, Hungarian), I was detailed to the 41st Royal Marine Commando (RMC). We were "assembled" in a tent camp near Southampton. The camp was surrounded by barbed wire, and that was the last contact we had with the outside world until D-Day. This segregation was imperative, because we were now slowly briefed about the details of the invasion. Though the real names of the area, towns or villages where we were supposed to land were never given to us, we got maps from which experts could have learned the actual location of the invasion.

Even the very plain girls who served us in the Canteen were not allowed to leave anymore. In the absence of other attractions, they became more beautiful every day.

These "camps" were an interesting experience from many points of view, but one experience was outstanding: General Montgomery came around and, among other things, made the point that after a landing, British troops get "beach happy", they just stay on the beaches too long and suffer too many casualties. That struck me as an important observation on the character of the British troops, who had such great admiration for their navy. This was a trap I was not going to fall into.

After dark on June 5th, we boarded small invasion crafts, each holding about 80 men. I believe we sailed in total darkness past the Isle of Wight together with hundreds of other boats, none of which showed any light - superb mastery of discipline and navigation. We were in the hull of these little boats, taking turns sitting on the steps to the deck, observing the surroundings and the approaching coast, and reporting our observations to the people below. It was cold, wet, and I refused to drink any alcohol (slows your instinctive reactions), but there was hot chocolate. Gradually, we could see the coast being lit up by our air attacks. An hour or two later, the German coastal guns were being trained on us and shells exploded near our boats.

When the boat slowed and the gang planks were let down, I ran into the water and waded ashore; anything to be away from such an obvious target.

There was a heavy smell of explosives drifting in a cloud over the beach, and there was what has been called the "cacophony of the devil," mortar and artillery shells whizzing and whining through the air. But the German fire was still largely directed at our ships and did not yet fall on the beach itself.

The beach was full of steel structures onto which the Germans had clamped huge artillery shells. These were supposed to act as tank traps, but these contraptions never worked. Members of the Corp of Engineers, who had landed before us, were busy blowing gaps into these steel barricades. Miraculously, they had ambushed a German Patrol of about 25 soldiers which had been sent out against them, and these Germans were now being herded into a spot about 100 yards from where I had come ashore. I ran over to them and my first thought was: "They look just like us German Jews; except for the different uniform, I would not be able to tell the difference between them and us German Jews". Then, holding my Tommy gun firmly but not too brazenly, I said: "Guten Morgen meine Herren, wo ist der Weg durch die Minenfelder?" (Good morning, gentlemen, where is the path through the minefields). They did not hesitate to point out the path through the minefields. I ran back, gathered up about a dozen people from 41st R. M Commando, anyone who was willing to follow me, and two minutes later, we were in Lion Sur Mere. Not one casualty, no more mortar fire.

More troops from 41st RMC gathered. We were supposed to take the German strongpoint at the other end of Lion Sur Mer, and slowly we made our way there along the main village road, which runs parallel to the beach. I had to scream at the troops to move forward by diving from one house into the next: a mortar or artillery shell falling onto a paved road would cause shrapnel to fly all along the road. At the entrance to the village we had passed the bodies of several British soldiers who obviously had been killed by such flying shrapnel. We had learned street fighting techniques in 3 Troop (as described above), but the Marines were "non blissfully" ignorant. The French readily opened their doors to us. In some houses there were civilians who had been hit. Pretty bad, no time to stop, could not spare our First Aid kits for them.

I had made up my mind that my first priority was to fight, infiltrate German lines and persuade the German soldiers to surrender. Tending to the injured whether soldiers or civilians, would have to wait until there was a short reprieve from fighting. Inhumane? Maybe, but then we were fighting the most inhumane war machine of modern times.

Then we came to the last row of houses before the strongpoint. By that time, we were well off the main road because there was sure to be a lookout in the strongpoint watching the road. These houses were empty, obviously had been empty for some time. I tried to find a spot from which I could overlook the strongpoint, but must have been noticed by a German sniper, who fired at me but missed. I rushed back into the lower part of the house. While we were milling around there, debating what to do next, we heard a very hefty explosion from the house next door. But, whatever missile was being fired was obviously aimed at the German strongpoint! Puzzling. We carefully entered the house and found an Arab (from Algeria, I believe) with an 1870/71 rifle, merrily firing into the German strongpoint. He had all the physical features (black hair, pronounced, bent nose, yellow skin) which the Nazi propaganda associated with Jews. Obviously he had been terribly maltreated by the Germans, and he was going to get "his own back". In my broken French I persuaded him to join us. Eventually, we gave him a Commando uniform and weapons. He stayed with us until December 1944, when he got injured in an accident. We lost track of him then; maybe the military hospital repatriated him to France.

The next incident may actually have happened before we met the Arab; I've lost track of the sequence of events. The Colonel of 41st RMC asked me to stick with him while he was going around checking the positions of the different Troops of 41st RMC (each "Commando" consisted of four or five "Troops"). The man carried only a briefcase, no weapons, and he would never lie down when we heard an artillery or mortar shell approaching. Utterly foolish. I sure ducked every time I had to; fighting yes, suicide no. (Next day, the Colonel was injured and he was out of the war).

We had surrounded the Lion Sur Mer strongpoint, which we were supposed to conquer immediately after landing. Some South African armored cars came up from the beach where we had landed earlier. The Colonel persuaded them to charge down the main Lion Sur Mer road, firing into the strongpoint and being followed by Y Troop of 41st RMC. An unwise decision; our maps showed that the road was covered by an anti-tank gun in a concrete bunker. The armored cars were shot up and lost, as was half of Y Troop. Naturally, I did not participate: fighting yes, suicide no. By that time, we could have attacked the strongpoint from the rear, using the armored cars only as hidden, mobile support guns. That's how we used Tanks and Armored cars in assaults for the rest of the European campaign.

41st RMC headquarters was then established on a farm just outside Lion Sur Mer and I was ordered there. I found myself a narrow space between two low stonewalls out in the open. We were bound to draw some mortar or artillery fire, and I did not want to take foolish risks. It was now going towards the evening and I was dead hungry. Between the walls, I cooked some of the dehydrated food we carried. I was also set to have a good, safe night's sleep. I could overlook some of the beaches from where we had come.

Just as it started to get dark, hundreds of Allied gliders were being pulled from England across the beachhead and being let loose further inland to land on the other side of the Orne Canal. A spectacular sight.

Then, out of nowhere came a German fighter plane, racing and twisting over the whole length of the beachhead. It says in the book "The Longest Day" that no one fired on it. Not true, he drew a lot of fire, but nobody hit him.

It was the end of D-Day, and we had accomplished none of our tasks: we had not taken the Lion Sur Mer strongpoint, we had not taken the German "headquarter" further inland, we had not linked up with 47RMC and the Americans in Luc Sur Mer, and we had lost half the Commando, mainly because the troops did not get off the beaches fast enough.

Next morning, the Colonel was injured, and 41st RMC was taken over by a Major who was the District Attorney of Liverpool - a "civilian", in contrast to the Colonel, who was a "professional". I was told to accompany the troops in an assault on the "headquarters," which, as I mentioned, was further inland. We decided to just run into the position without covering fire and take everyone by surprise. It worked! This was not the sort of fortified headquarters we besieged and successfully assaulted a week or two later. No, this had been a temporary headquarters of some infantry battalion, hastily sent as reinforcement from the Russian Front. The battalion had already withdrawn, leaving behind an ethnic German rearguard (Volga Deutsche?) from Eastern Europe, whose German I could hardly understand. They were only too happy to surrender, but they proved useless for intelligence on our next target.

I was supposed to turn around and join the Troop, which was going into the strongpoint, but I didn't get there in time: the strongpoint surrendered without much of a fight. Very soon thereafter, we were in Luc Sur Mer. End of the D-Day assignments. Start of a totally new chapter.

## Onwards from D-Day

Having been in Luc Sur Mer for two days, I was ordered to accompany one of the Troops of 41 R. M. Commando, which moved south further into the beachhead. We quartered ourselves on a well-kept estate, whose owner was an attractive woman about 35 years old. She had a magnificent presence, cheerful, energetic, a sportive body, black hair, a slightly aquiline nose and a quick intelligence. We soon referred to her as "La Contessa". She told us that her husband was a Colonel in the French Army and that he had been a prisoner of war in Germany since 1940. She ran the estate with only one permanent maid, a woman of about fifty years old.

We had arrived late in the afternoon and immediately proceeded to patrol the surroundings, going deeper into the beachhead to assure ourselves that there would be no nasty surprises from German patrols. We were at the border between the British and American sectors, but we seemed to be all alone, not a sign of the presence of Allied or German armies. We came across three dead Waffen SS soldiers, probably killed by American paratroopers, who had landed in this vicinity on D-Day. There were also a lot of dead cows. During the daylight hours the area was eerily quiet.

The lady of the estate told us that there had been sporadic German shelling during the nights ever since D-Day; after posting some guards around the estate, we examined the house and came to the conclusion that the slightly sunken kitchen with its very sturdy walls would provide adequate protection, barring a direct hit, and we told the lady and her maid to make that kitchen her quarters for the night. They also brought a magnificent German shepherd dog into this shelter.

Our precautions proved highly warranted: after dark at about 11 p. m., the German artillery bombardment started, and we were obviously its target. We had come with one 15-ton truck and two or three jeeps; somehow a German artillery observer must have regarded that as a major troop movement, because we were really "getting it". It was almost worse than D-Day, except that it was simply artillery fire with no silent mortar fire mixed into it.

The poor maid went "bomb happy." She was in a total panic, screaming and wanting to run out, certain prescription for getting hurt. We restrained her forcibly, pinning her down on the floor. The dog, too, went into a total panic, yowling and whining at a deafening noise level. I had not realized that dogs could go "bomb happy".

But "La Contessa" was totally unfazed: she never lost her calm, her smile or her aristocratic bearing; she was forever encouraging us in whatever we had to do to keep safe and avoid surprises by German patrols. I really admired her. Between the pre-D-Day Allied bombardment, the paratrooper landings and the nightly German artillery fire, she had probably seen as much warfare as her husband saw in 1940.

The artillery bombardment had not caused much damage; the house was not at all hit. In the morning we invited the two ladies to have breakfast with us, but we could not offer them coffee, since the British Army rations did not contain coffee.

At noon we had to move on, rejoining the rest of the Commando unit.

# The Siege of the Underground Radar Stations

Next day, we moved from the estate which was just South of Luc Sur Mer, further into the Normandy beachhead, closer to the "front", which at that moment was pretty stationary. The initial German counterattacks had exhausted themselves, and the Allies were in the process of consolidating their positions in the beachhead, landing massive equipment and additional armored divisions. Also, they were building up supply depots for ammunition, gasoline and whatever else would be needed to mount offensives out of the beachhead. There were endless convoys on even the smallest roads, and at that moment, the chances of being hurt in a traffic accident were greater than getting hurt in fighting.

The initial advance had bypassed a heavily fortified German radar station, including two interconnected underground, networks of "bunkers", called the Moltke and the Hindenburg after the WWI generals who, in the distorted nationalistic German history of the outbreak of WWI, had successfully "defended" the fatherland. The fact that these radar stations had been given these revered names convinced me that they were of major importance to the German defense system.

41 R. M. Commando was assigned to besiege these stations, which were surrounded by two extensive barbed wire systems enclosing 300-meter- wide minefields. Also on the north side, the side from which an invader was likely to come, the barbed wire minefield system was protected by an antitank ditch (stupid WWI tactical thinking). We were to display maximum aggressiveness, convincing the Germans that they were facing a huge army, not just 400 lightly equipped troops. Our forward positions were just outside the barbed wire minefield system. We had to crawl into those positions so as to avoid being seen by the Germans, but further back we were housed in some prefab barracks, probably used to house the slave labor which built these fortifications. Life there could have been quite comfortable but for the fact that only a kilometer away, the Allies were hastily building a new airfield. Almost every night, German guns from the front (not from the radar stations) were pounding the airfield, and in the language of the marines, "we were catching the shorts."

Our main positions were on the west side of the underground fortifications. Their minefields, on that side ran from north to south. Between their lines and ours was a slight elevation of the ground which hid us from their view, provided that we were crawling. or lying low. We expected that all their machine gun positions were connected by deep trenches, so they could move more easily. One day a big hare run along the ridge between the lines. Both sides started firing, but nobody hit the hare.

For the second night of the siege it was decided to get a look at the inside of these stations. My Three Troup colleagues, Sgt Major O' Neil and Maurice Latimer, were to go with 4 or 5 marines inside the Hindenburg and I was to take two marines into the Moltke.

I have often been asked, "Weren't you scared to death to take on such assignments?" Yes I was. I composed farewell letters to friends, girlfriend and family and gave them to one of the marines for mailing if I did not come back. Yes, I was scared to death until we actually left our lines. After that, the concentration had to be all on technique, no time for fear.

I had convinced myself that I had worked out a safe and rapid way to get across a minefield; elementary physics $(t=s/v)$ indicates that crawling is too slow to be viable. We had to walk with one hand on the ground, making sure that we put our feet and weight only on a hard smooth surface. Laying a mine disturbs the surface; such disturbances were to be avoided. This mode of self-propulsion required utter fitness, unencumbered by alcohol.

We left our lines and went straight to the first barbed wire fence of the minefield and carefully cut our way through the barbed wire, causing minimum disturbance of this outer fence.

In no more than 30 minutes, we crossed the 300-meter-wide minefield and arrived at the much more formidable second barbed wire fence, which separated the minefield from the system of fortifications and underground bunkers of the Moltke. I carefully examined the barbed wire to discover electrified lines; there were none, so we proceeded to cut a small gap through this fence.

The night was still; I was praying for the German artillery from the beach- head front to start pounding the airfield. No such luck. It was eerily still and we were right inside a German strongpoint. We came across several fortified machinegun positions. They were not manned. We saw the huge steel doors which led into the bunker. They were completely below ground level. A wide ditch led into them, wide enough to allow the entrance of motorized equipment.

It was obvious that the Germans had "closed down" for the night, safely hiding in this impenetrable mass of reinforced concrete. But then we heard the whining of a dog, probably on a chain, quite agitated. I was afraid the dog would suddenly jump at us. What to do? Our

Three Troop training had taught us to use a certain chemical to put off watch dogs, but of course, I didn't have that chemical. Give our position away by shooting the dog? Out of the question; that would be suicidal. We didn't even have a Commando knife between the three of us to slit the throat of that dog.

Anyhow, I felt that we had seen enough. The three of us were not supposed to conquer the strong point. It was time to withdraw. We carefully restored the barbed wire, crossed the minefield and got back to our positions.

In the meantime, Maurice Latimer had similarly made his way into the Hindenburg. He came across one of the fortified machine gun positions, and saw the helmet of a German soldier. He hit the man just below the helmet with his pistol, only to find that the helmet was just supported on a piece of wood. Unfortunately, he caught his finger between the pistol and the piece of wood, and he badly bruised his hand. He did not report this injury because he did not want to be sent home, but he bandaged it up himself.

Two nights later, it was decided that I was to take about 15 marines and an officer into the strongpoint. We were to occupy some of the fortified machine gun positions, and in the morning, when the Germans emerged from their underground fortification, we were to create enough havoc to get them to surrender.

Once more, we crossed the minefield at the spot where we had previously cut the barbed wire. Again I carefully felt for hard ground. I had taught the minefield crossing technique to all those who followed me, nevertheless I had also given strict orders that the marine behind me was to carefully put his feet only on the spots where I had put my feet, and the same discipline of positioning feet was to be maintained by everyone in the patrol.

Having crossed about ¾ of the minefield, I discovered a newly placed shoe-mine. They look like partially opened cigar boxes and I had almost put my hand right into it. I told the marine who followed me to stop while I investigated. 10 yards or so further along I discovered another shoe mine. From there on, the path was clear to the inside barbed wire fence. I put a white handkerchief on the mine nearest to the fence, then went back and whispered into everyone's ear. "There are two shoe mines ahead; I put a white handkerchief on one of them and my hand will be on the other. Proceed to the barbed wire fence. There are no more mines." The patrol proceeded. Suddenly there was a muffled explosion and a well suppressed cry of someone getting hurt. I judged that someone had set off an antipersonnel mine, the type that jumps into the air and then explodes to spray a mass of shrapnel. I rolled over into a minute depression, waiting for the second explosion and expecting to get a lot of shrapnel into my back. The second explosion came but I was unhurt. I got up, still moving with one hand on the ground, to find out what had happened.

The patrol had "frozen," lying on the ground expecting German machine gun fire, but there was no reaction from the strongpoint.

What had happened? One of the marines had stepped on my handkerchief, setting off the shoe mine. His leg was severely injured. Then the other shoe mine, on which I had had my hand, had gone off, either by sympathetic detonation or because the mines were interconnected. Had I been lucky!

We decided that we had probably alerted the Germans and that it was unwise to go on. The officer took the patrol back, and I stayed behind with one very strong sergeant and the injured marine.

The sergeant put the marine across his shoulders while I carefully guided his feet to slowly work our way across the minefield. We tried to give the injured marine a morphine injection, but we did not succeed. Probably, I had not pierced the seal of the syringe correctly or the syringe was defective. Anyhow, the marine passed out.

It took us two hours to get through the minefield. Medical orderlies with a stretcher and the Commando doctor were waiting for us at the edge of the minefield.

I returned to our billet in the laborer's huts. I had a beautiful breast pocket bottle, which was originally filled with navy rum, but in the course of the days, as I had drunk from it I had topped it with the very crude distilled apple cider which was readily available in Normandy. A horrible mixture, but now I emptied the whole bottle in one go. I was super agitated, but I wanted to go to sleep. There were only three hours left before the five o'clock standby.

I felt bad about the patrol. We had been stupid to cross the minefield at exactly the same spot where we had crossed two nights before; I could have found a half dozen other paths to cross. But the marines did not see it that way: they were most impressed that I had stuck with the sergeant, guiding his feet for two hours and getting him and the injured marine back to our lines without further incident. That's what I loved about the British: when things went wrong, nobody cast around for blame, but everybody saw only the positive side. The marine who lost his leg even sent me a letter of thanks from his hospital in England.

It wasn't all work and no play in those days. Since we were "out" almost every night, Maurice

Latimer and I had convinced our superiors that we could take off every afternoon. So the afternoon after my misfired patrol, we hitchhiked back to Luc Sur Mer, where several Cafés had reopened. The day was warm and sunny, and we sat in the open-air part of a Cafe and indulged ourselves in aperitifs, which were totally new to me. Twice I went back to the estate of the Contessa to flirt with her. She was very happy to see me, but she also knew where to draw the line.

Two nights after the misfired patrol we were "out" again. This time a Petard tank was put at our disposal. I was supposed to guide the tank to the edge of the antitank ditch at the north side of the Moltke fortifications. From there a petard, which has a range of about 400 yards, would be fired to hit the main bunker of the strongpoint. At the same time, another patrol was to enter the Hindenburg. Sgt. Major O'Neil, who was an explosives expert, had persuaded the Commando Officer in Command that a Bangalore torpedo (300 meters long!) should be pushed through the minefield to create a path for the patrol.

I left our lines with just one marine and made my way through the corridor between the minefields and the airfield under construction. I had carefully surveyed that whole area when we first arrived to besiege these strongpoints. In daylight the Germans would have been able to see us. At that moment, all hell broke loose:

German guns from the beachhead front were pounding away at the airfield, and many shells were falling short into the corridor. We took cover as best as we could; impossible to go forward. While being pinned down, I was somewhat amused: in our Three Troop training, the Skipper had always emphasized, "No matter what, you can not be late for a combat appointment," and here I was, late for the third time for a combat appointment.

When the artillery fire ceased, we quickly made our way to the agreed spot, where the tank was waiting for us. The officer in charge of the tank had realized that we were pinned down by the artillery fire.

We had brought several rolls of white tape. I said, "From here we will roll out the tape to the edge of the antitank ditch. Drive the tank so that the tape is in the center of your tracks; I can't guarantee that there might not be some antitank mines on the side, but this path is clear. We will mark the edge of the antitank ditch with another white tape. Be careful not to drive past it."

All went well. The tank got to the edge of the ditch. We hid behind it, partly because we expected the Germans to fire antitank guns and partly because we had learned that these 300-pound petard missiles occasionally fall short.

The tank fired two missiles. They hit with thunderous explosions. We all waited for the

German reaction: there was none. Suddenly the tank crew decided to drive along the edge of the antitank ditch to find alternate positions. Probably they were following standard instructions not to fire more than two shots from the same position. Before we realized what they were doing, the tank had fallen into the ditch. It was off its tracks, but not quite upside down. The crew got out unharmed. We helped them to scramble up the steep embankment of the antitank ditch and told them to keep their heads down; but for the very dark night we were in full view of the Germans, and we all made our way back to the original meeting place. In typical British fashion, we all just said, "Bad luck." The tank could not be "rescued" until the strongpoint was taken and cranes could be brought in, and so we parted company.

In the meantime, at the Hindenburg, the patrol had pushed the 300-meter-long Bangalore Torpedo into the minefield, as suggested by Sgt Major O'Neill. Maurice Latimer lit the fuse and then scrambled to a position from which he could safely observe the effects. The explosion ripped through the minefield, setting off some mines, but Maurice realized that the forward part of the torpedo, nearer to the inner fence, had not exploded. Keeping his head low, he quickly made his way along the path marked out by the torpedo's explosion. He relit the unexploded portion of the torpedo, but the bandage of his hand, injured in one of the previous patrols (an injury which he had never reported), caught fire and he got badly burned.

The second explosion elicited heavy machine-gun fire from the strongpoint. Maurice managed to get out without any further harm, but "the game was up" and the venture was called off.

The Commando doctor insisted that Maurice be flown home, very much against Maurice's will. He rejoined us only in October, just before the Walcheren landings.

A few days later, we were finally given enough hardware to make a final assault in daylight. Again, I was assigned to the "Moltke", my specialty.

A Flail tank made a path through the minefield and we rushed in. We had to make sure that there were no Germans outside the underground fortifications. There were none. Then another tank brought a very heavy pointed charge, which a Royal Engineers officer set up on top of the underground bunker. These pointed charges can drill holes through reinforced concrete. At that point, I discovered a periscope sticking up from the bunker. I felt we were being observed. I kicked in the glass and was going to stick a phosphorous hand grenade into it, which I would have exploded with a shot from my Tommy gun. I hoped that the burning phosphorous would run down into the underground fortification, but the Royal Engineers officer told me to take cover; he was ready to explode his charge. He got back into his tank, and we took cover in one of the machine gun positions. A loud explosion followed, but almost no shrapnel. The pointed charge had done its job, drilling a hole into or through the concrete.

There was no immediate reaction from the occupants of the underground fortifications, and the Engineers got ready to set a second charge. But at that moment the huge underground doors opened just slightly, and a white flag was pushed through the slit. I shouted, "Kommen Sie heraus und ergeben Sie sich," slowly, about 150 Germans filed out. (Years later, I saw a rendition of this whole attack on an underground fortification with huge electrically operated doors, in a fictional American movie.)

I never had time to go into the underground fortification because I tried to find the highest ranking German officer to "persuade" him to go with me to the "Hindenburg" to get its crew to surrender. This proved unnecessary; an additional 300 German soldiers were quickly emerging from that fortification. We collected them all on the road which led out of our positions.

The 41st Royal Marine Commando Commanding Officer came by and said, "This crowd has to be taken to the POW camps on the beaches before nightfall." He detailed an officer and about 15 other ranks to lead the prisoners. I said, "Leave it to me." From a little hill on the side of the road I shouted commands in German to get the whole crew to "fall in." These commands I had NOT learned in Three Troop; they were part of the militaristic upbringing of the 5 years of public high school to which I had been exposed after Hitler came to power in Germany.

My commands were followed with an alacrity which astonished both me and the marines. "Left turn, quick march, follow the Green Beret soldiers in front." Three hour's march to the D-Day beaches.

Sotte Voce the marines were singing.

"When the Fuhrer says we is the master race Sieg Heil, Sieg Heil, right in the Fuehrer's face. Not too loud, because the Fuehrer's in disgrace Sieg Heil, Sieg Heil right in the Fuehrer's face."

"And when Old Goering says they never bomb this place, Sieg Heil, Sieg Heil, right in Old Goering's face, but not too loud because Old Goering is in disgrace Sieg Heil, Sieg Heil, right in Old Goering's face"

There were a lot more unprintable verses to this ditty.

On the way to the beaches, we met a British armored brigade which had just landed. The tank crews stopped and looked out of their hatches to see this long line of German soldiers. They shouted, "Where did you get that numb lot?" "Did you leave any for us?" Some jumped down from their tanks, slapped our backs, shouting, "Good old Commandos,"; no doubt this encounter lifted their morale considerably.

## Diversion

As I said before, since our "work" was almost exclusively in the hours of darkness, we had persuaded the authorities that we should have the afternoon off. But after Maurice Latimer was injured, I was pretty much left to my own devices: Swinton had been shipped back to England two or three days after D-Day because of constant headaches, possibly brought on by shell shock on D-Day and Sgt Major O'Neill spent almost all his time with the officers of 41 Commando. He was very caring whenever I ran into him, but, apart from very short discussions just before going out on patrols, I saw very little of him.

The day after we lost the petard tank in the antitank ditch and Maurice Latimer was flown back to England because of his burn injury, I decided to hitchhike to the church in Amfreville, where members of Three Troop met to exchange experiences. On the way there, I came across a new cemetery, and for some unknown reason, I asked the jeep which had picked me up to stop, and I went into the cemetery. There I discovered the graves of the Three Troop members Franklyn, Laddy and Webster. In spite of the fact that we all wore dog tags on which it said CoE (Church of England), I was pretty shocked to find that their graves were marked with crosses. The world, and particularly the French, whom we had liberated and whose soil now was the last resting place for these Three Troop members, had to know that we were Jewish! I shuddered to think that my own grave would be marked in that fashion.

I continued to hitchhike to the church in Amfreville and as expected, found a gathering of Three Troop members. Stewart told me the details of the Skipper's (Hilton Jone's) patrol, in which the Skipper had been injured and taken prisoner. Someone argued that better preparation and a bit more patience could have given that patrol a better chance for success (from the details I heard later, I doubt it). Shelley recounted the circumstances of the death of Arlen, with the lesson that you don't fight when you are angry (just like in tennis; calm yourself down first). Bartlett was arguing with his best friend Lawrence, who was scheduled to go out that night and take a prisoner. Lawrence, whose political views were very leftish, had no faith in British officers; he was going to take a patrol of "other ranks" only, to give him covering fire in case he got into trouble. Bartlett argued. "They won't know when to fire, where to fire and how to fire," but Lawrence was unconvinced. I was told much later by one of the sergeants who was on that patrol that his patrol did not lay down covering fire when Lawrence got into trouble and was taken prisoner, never to be seen again. Maybe it would not have helped, but the attempt should have been made.

Next day, I wrote a letter to Langley, the administrative officer of Three Troop, to make him aware of the location of the graves of Franklyn, Laddie and Webster. Langley informed the next of kin of my discovery. Of course, I knew Mrs. Laddie, because she was an Aberdovey young lady. I got an emotional letter back from her; she was expecting a child. I also got a sad letter from Franklyn's parents. Franklyn had been with 41st R. M. Commando in the invasion of Sicily, and since I now was with 41st R. M. Commando, his parents assumed that I had been with their son all the time. Unfortunately, I hardly knew him, but I tried my best to respond to both these letters in a compassionate way.

Once a month we were allowed to write a letter, which was not censored by our own officers, but it went to some War Department station, where the censors did not know us personally but judged the letters solely on possible military intelligence content. Via my cover address, I sent such a letter to my brother, making him aware that the graves of all the fallen from Three Troop would have crosses, though most of us were Jews. My brother lived in an orthodox Jewish rooming house (pension), where one of his roommates was a young Rabbi who was the Secretary of the Board of Governors, the organization which governs most of the Jewish Congregations in the U. K. The young Rabbi promised to make it his business to rectify the markings of the graves after the war.

Roll forward to 1947. Anita had come from the US to England, and we had gotten engaged. I took her to Aberdovey to show her the beauty of the place where we had been reborn. After having spent two months in war-dreary Manchester, where I studied, that was a welcome change for her.

In a tearoom I saw a little girl who looked the spitting image of Max Laddie. I asked her for her name, and she replied, "Maxine Laddy." It turned out that her mother owned the tearoom. When her mother came in, I told her who I was, or rather who I had been. She found it hard to reminisce; she had been 35 or more when she met and married Max Laddie, who was a sweet and warm person. Her "married bliss" had lasted just too short a time.

After a few days in Aberdovey, Anita and I spent a night in a hotel in Harlech. When we came down for breakfast next morning, there was only one elderly couple in the breakfast room. They talked to each other softly, but with a strong German accent. I was sure they were Franklyn's parents, sadly visiting the beautiful area where their son had been trained. But I didn't have the heart to tell them who I was; it would have been an emotional experience for them, but to this day I regret my inaction.

Roll forward to sometime in the '80s, I visited Washington, D. C., regularly as a member of a high-powered government committee judging processes for synthetic gas. One afternoon, I met Peter Masters in a little park before rushing back to the airport. Peter had been in Normandy for the D-Day anniversary celebration. He showed me pictures, and there in one of them was Franklyn's grave, now marked with a Magen David (Star of David).

# The Hedgerow War

The underground radar stations had been in the area of Douvres/La Deliverand. They were almost near the borderline of the British and American sectors, the western part of the British sector, while the main actions of the British army were at the eastern and southeastern part of the Normandy beachhead.

After the surrender of the radar stations, we moved to the northeastern tip of the beachhead at Sallnelles, where a swamp separated us from the German positions which were part of the "Atlantic Wall". From these concrete emplacements, retractable guns could fire into the floating harbors which were the Allies' only supply lifeline.

Creeping to the edge of the swamp in daylight, we could see the German emplacement. On rare occasions, we saw one of the retractable guns, sticking out its barrel and firing at shipping or at the floating harbors. We could also see the farmhouse in the swamp which Three Troop's Sergeant Fuller (von Kargerer Stein) had used as his observation post to direct American fighter bombers in their attempt to destroy the German gun emplacements. Unfortunately, one bomb had fallen short in these low-level attacks and had killed Fuller. For these attacks the bomb fins were sawn off so the bomb would continue to streak parallel to the ground after it was released. Thus, a bomb released slightly too early would hit any obstacle in its way.

Fuller - an Austrian secondhand car salesman, who, proverbially, would sell you his grandmother and you would happily walk away thinking that you had bought a bus - was attached to 47 R. M. Commando. All their landing ships were sunk on D-Day, and they had landed in Luc Sur Mer with almost nothing but their clothes. But Fuller walked into the nearest German strongpoint and convinced the crew that they had no chance to survive and that they should surrender, which they did.

For all that and for his guidance of the American fighter bombers, Fuller was recommended for the posthumous award of the Victoria Cross, which would have given his widow a substantially higher pension. But because he was not a British citizen, he got nothing.

After all these efforts, the annoying German guns were still in place.

For us, Sallnelles meant mosquitoes, mortar bombs and a lot of dangerous patrols. My section stayed in a large farmhouse, which had already taken a few artillery or bomb hits, but at least its ground level was dry. The mosquitoes were so annoying that we had to sleep in full clothing and use our camouflage nets as mosquito nets to cover our faces. Several times at dusk we would shoot flamethrowers into thick swarms of mosquitoes, but we were told to stop that because we were giving away our position.

Every morning at dawn, about 5 a. m., we had to "stand by," meaning that we had to get into defensive positions with our weapons ready for action, on the theory that the enemy could have infiltrated our position during the hours of darkness and would swing into full attack at dawn. To me the "stand by" was particularly annoying, because often I did not come back from patrol until 2 a. m. and by the time we could "stand down" it was time to organize some breakfast.

These conditions were wearisome; I needed my sleep in the afternoon, and while we were at Sallanells, I never took a "liberty ride."

Occasionally, we were subjected to German mortar attacks, but we were now backed by Allied artillery, only too keen to find targets and silence these mortars. We were told that 800 guns could be brought onto an "oxo" (maximum importance) target, a concentration of firepower unique in the history of warfare.

This too was the time when the "armored fist punches" about which Montgomery had talked before D-Day came into play: 1000 bombers carpet bombing on a narrow front three miles wide and five miles deep, followed by an attack by hundred of tanks. But all that happened on the southern front of the beachhead; breaking out to the east, at our front, would have meant rolling up the Atlantic Wall and its extension, too costly a task.

To go from the farmhouse to our forward positions, where we started our patrols into "no man's land," we walked along a series of hedgerows, until aerial reconnaissance sent us a picture showing a well worn path along those hedges, so we had to find different routes.

On most of my night patrols I was accompanied by only two other men. Frequently, one of them was an officer who had just come from the UK - since, we had lost half the unit on D-Day - and one "other rank," a corporal or a marine. The officer was under strict instructions to let me lead, since I was so much more experienced.

Two of these patrols were remarkable.

## Pinned Down For The Night

The first patrol was made up of eight men, including Sgt Major O'Neil of Three Troop and we set out in the early evening, when it was still light, to find the exact position of the German line. As usual, we carefully spied out open fields from behind hedges. Then I left the patrol behind the hedge, in cover, while I crawled or "ducked" across the open field. After several such advances, I came under heavy machine gun fire. I could feel the bullets churning up the ground around me, but I had rolled into a shallow depression and I was probably not visible anymore. The machine gun fire stopped. I knew I could not move until it was dark, and I rightly assumed that our patrol had withdrawn. As soon as it got dark, a German patrol came out of their lines carefully working their way on the far side of a hedgerow which ran perpendicular to the row where I had left the rest of our patrol. There seemed to be three German soldiers, and they set up a machinegun twenty yards from me. Since I could not see them and since I expected them still to be "covered" by the machinegun that had originally fired on me, I decided to just lie still.

During the night I heard the hissing snake sound which was the Three Troop signal for establishing communication. O'Neil had obviously returned to look for me, but I could not return the signal because of the closeness of the German patrol. I hoped that he and whoever was with him would withdraw; I was sure I could get back on my own.

Once during the night I had to urinate. I had never done that lying down. I was surprised at how much noise it made. Villiers from Three Troop told me that he had once been in the same position and he thought he had a major waterfall on his hand.

Just before dawn the German patrol withdrew, so I carefully rolled over to the hedge behind which I had left our patrol. From there I slowly made my way back into our lines, making sure I would not be shot at by our outposts.

When I came to our first outpost, the corporal in charge said, "I was expecting you. I was told that you had been hit and had disappeared, but I said not that bloke (guy); he'll come back hale and hardy in the morning."

By the time I came back to our main position, it was well past the stand by time. After I had reported to O'Neil and Colonel Palmer, it was time for an inspection by one of the Commando generals who had come over from London. I had not even had a chance to take off the black face-paint which we wore when we went into action. (Remember, we never wore helmets, but covered our green berets with camouflage netting the size of a generous scarf).

Palmer introduced me to the general, saying, "This is Corporal Gray from Three Troop 10 Commando; he was pinned down by German machine guns all night and we thought we had lost him, but he made it back this morning." The general said to me, "I think you are really enjoying it." (He was sufficiently high up in the Commando Command to know the real identity or background of Three Troop members.) I said,

"This is what we came here for, so we might as well do our best."

My experience on that patrol had some dire consequences: the following day Colonel Palmer told me to go over to the headquarters of 47 R. M. Commando, since the colonel of that Commando doubted my story. At 47 Commando I was thoroughly interrogated by the second in command and the intelligence officer in the presence of a few other officers, including the colonel, who sat in the background. When his staff had finished questioning me, he came forward and said very sharply, "I am convinced there are no Germans in that area." To which I replied very firmly, "I can't tell you who is in that area now. There certainly were Germans there the night before last."

A day or two later, 47 Commando sent out a "Single File" patrol into an adjacent area, probably to find out the real location of the German line. In such patrols the group moves as a body, in single file, each member being assigned a fixed field of vision, pointing his loaded weapon in that direction.

This type of a patrol might be useful in mobile warfare, but it was totally inapplicable in the fixed-line position warfare in which we were engaged, where enemy lines had to be approached either by stealth (silent infiltration) or by a frontal attack. As a result, the patrol, which included Three Troop's Peter Terry, was totally wiped out, every member killed or injured. When darkness fell, Peter Terry was rescued by Three Troop's Ian Harris, a very brave man who had heard about this disaster. Peter Terry was seriously injured and had to be discharged from the army.

## Our Own Artillery

The other remarkable patrol of our stay around Sallnelles involved a still more harassing experience.

I was accompanied by an inexperienced officer, who had just joined 41 Commando, and a Marine Corporal. Once more, we were supposed to locate the exact German line and possibly stumble across a German patrol. In total darkness we worked our way along and across the usual hedgerows until, surprisingly, we came across an open field. While carefully crossing that field, I suddenly realized that we were in a minefield. There and then, in the dark, whispering into their ears, I had to instruct the officer and the corporal in the technique I used for crossing minefields: one hand on the ground, put you feet only on firm earth. All went well and we thought we had come to the end of the minefield, when suddenly our own artillery was firing onto this minefield and possibly the German positions just beyond it.

This was the most frightening experience I had during the whole war, because I realized that the shrapnel from the exploding shells was traveling parallel to the ground, while all the German artillery shells to which I had been exposed so far threw their shrapnel largely into the air. I had learned enough about "lifting" and "shaped" explosives to identify the cause of our distress, but that helped very little. But with this bombardment in progress, there was no need to proceed silently. In a normal voice I told the officer and the corporal to roll into depressions and wait there for a let up in the barrage. Since this situation was so utterly unexpected, we gradually withdrew to our own lines.

When we got back, the officer said to me, "Go to bed, Corporal, I'll take care of the report." He was deliriously happy. I hoped that he would write the report in such a way as to get a medal for this patrol. It would be well deserved. Fancy being caught by your own artillery in an enemy minefield as your baptism of fire! The discovery of that minefield was regarded as valuable.

## Troan

From the most northeasterly point of the Normandy beachhead, we were eventually moved to the most southeasterly point, close to Troan. This position was "active" by day and by night: German mortar and artillery fire would come down on us at irregular but frequent intervals, with almost no warning because their mortar and artillery positions were so close to us. When we heard the firing of the guns or mortars, the shells had practically arrived.

Our position had previously been occupied by a regiment of the Guards, and they had dug deep, steep and clean trenches and foxholes. There had been many more Guardsmen than there now were Marine Commandos, so we each had a choice of foxholes for our "personal quarters." Each of these foxholes was about six feet long, two feet wide and 41/2 feet deep. Eventually, we even covered them with planks and earth to protect ourselves against rain and direct mortar hits. But in spite of all this "comfort" and protection, it was impossible to sleep during these bombardments, and we never got a night or a day of rest. This was World War I warfare all over again.

Of course we could not spend all our time in our foxholes, but when we were out of them we had to "hurry along", keeping our heads low.

This was the time when the deadliest blow was delivered to the German Army in Normandy. Though we were not acquainted with the overall tactic, we were sufficiently close to the action to hear the continuous drones of hundreds of airplanes, and to follow it on one of our unit radio sets. We knew something special was going on.

Once again, hundreds of airplanes "carpet" bombed a narrow part of the front 3-5 miles wide, 3 miles deep. Then the Allied tanks rolled in, but we noticed from the radio transmissions that they were not meeting much resistance.

A few hours later, another wave of hundreds of planes was coming over for another carpet bombing attack. A day or two later, we learned what had happened: the Germans had more or less withdrawn from the area of the first carpet bombing. Instead, two and one half divisions of the Waffen SS were readied for a massive counter attack to cut right through the whole beachhead. But aerial surveillance had spotted the movements of these SS divisions. The second wave of carpet bombing had caught them out in the open: most of them died from the excess pressure or from the lack of oxygen created by the carpet bombing. These divisions never appeared again. They were not reconstituted.

Again, while in the Troan region I regularly went out on night patrols. In a way, the patrols were easier than they had been at Sallnelles because the German lines were much closer. Once we thought a German patrol was coming in our direction; we fired at them and were surprised when no fire was returned. Eventually I knew the exact location of the German lines.

Then one night the word came through that the Germans had withdrawn. So at dawn we went into what had been Troan. There was not even the shell of a single house left in the town; only massive electric and telephone wires on the streets attested to the former settlement.

We hung around the town all day. Apparently, no decision had been made as yet about hot pursuit. In the evening I was thinking that it would be nice to spend just one night in our comfortable foxholes without interruption by mortar and artillery fire. Others must have had the same thought: we were ordered to return to our previous positions where we could cook and sleep in comfort for just one night.

Next day, a different warfare began: we were on the move. The Normandy beachhead was now part of history.

# Pont L'Eveque

We had been on the move for five nights in succession since the Germans started to pull back from the southeastern corner of the Normandy beachhead. We never met any resistance during these night moves, because we never moved along any roads. Colonel Palmer, the C. O of 41 R. M. Commando, believed that moving along roads would entail considerable casualties. Thus, we carefully moved across country from one row of hedges to the next, most of the time in single file. I understood that we were just told where we had to be by the next morning. The path was not specified, but after getting his orders, Colonel Palmer called in his staff and a route avoiding roads was agreed upon on the maps. From then on, the Adjutant had to lead. He had a tiny flashlight to help him read the maps. He had to steer us by compass and the contours of the countryside. In Three Troop I was regarded as a pretty competent map-reader, but I could not have matched the Adjutant's feat.

All the fighting we saw during that time took place when we did move during daytime. One time, in the early evening, I was with A Troop and we had spread out to advance across a field with thick hedgerows on all sides. Captain Stevens, Troop Commander of A Troop, was well ahead of his troops. Suddenly, I saw a German standing up behind one of the hedges on our side, lifting his rifle to fire at Captain Stevens. He must have been completely drunk to stand up like that. He had not seen me; two bullets from my Tommy gun made him roll over backwards. Expecting more German soldiers, we changed the direction of our advance immediately towards the slightly elevated hedgerow behind which the German had appeared. There, we came across a dirt road leading to a village. Two girls in fine dresses came out of the village. They were not at all surprised to see us. Later on, I realized that this must have been a Sunday. I asked them in French, "Where are the Germans?" They explained that most of them had left, but that there were a few with a gun near the church further down the road. We got off the road immediately, set on finding the church while moving from hedgerow to hedgerow. Peeping through an elevated hedgerow, I saw three German soldiers about to scuttle a gun. I got everyone to duck: the explosion would set splinters flying in all directions, but immediately after the detonation we rushed in and overwhelmed the Germans before they had a chance to pick up their personal weapons.

The subsequent night move was strenuous but uneventful. The following day we moved again, this time largely on small roads. No resistance, but the physical strain proved too much for some Marine Commandos, who were transported by jeep and one light truck which followed us. In the evening we arrived at a farm which overlooked Pont L'Eveque. A steady barrage of artillery fire, mortars and machine guns could be heard from there. There is a mountain range on each side of Pont L'Eveque. We were on one of these ranges, and the German artillery was on the range across town.

I was in the vegetable garden of the farmhouse when I heard artillery shells coming at me. I threw myself flat on the ground, but when a shell exploded close to me, something hit the sole of my boot, leaving me without any feeling in my foot. When the shelling stopped, I limped into the farmhouse where our doctor had set up a First Aid station. The doctor's examination showed that there was no damage to my foot, just a temporary numbness. Probably the exploding shell had thrown a stone against my foot. I found myself a secure place to catch up on my sleep.

Next morning, the cacophony of the devil had increased, when Colonel Palmer asked me to go with him into Pont L'Eveque. We were going to drive at high speed by jeep along a sunken road which was obviously under the observation of the Germans, hoping that we could disappear into the streets of Pont L'Eveque before the Germans had a chance to zero their guns onto the road.

We reached the town without incident. One of the troops of 41 R. M. Commando was already in town. British paratroopers had moved into the town the previous day. We learned that the Germans were mainly around the railway station, that there was a square before the railway station, but that the houses on our side of the square were probably not occupied by the Germans. We carefully moved through the town. The paratroopers had set up three-inch mortars in the churchyard of a solidly built church. There they were relatively safe from the German artillery. They were feeding their mortars furiously in order to force the Germans to keep their heads down and give us a chance to get to the railway station square. It was a beautiful, sunny day, but the air was laden with dust and smoke, and any move along the roads would draw sniper or machine gun fire.

We reached the houses on our side of the square, but now every move we made drew a hail of machine gun fire. We, too, had to fire at anything that moved: we were scared that the Germans would position an antitank gun to fire at us point blank. Their rearguards usually had antitank guns, but the walls of the houses in which we took cover were not sufficiently sturdy to protect us from an antitank shell.

We never managed to find a position for our own 3" mortars. The 2" mortars were regarded as suicide weapons, I doubt that we had any with us. Colonel Palmer *went* to see the commanders of the other units, which were battling in Pont L'Eveque, but he left us a major asset: the faithful signaler. This Marine never carried a weapon, or even food or drinks. He just lugged a very heavy two-way radio set. He treated it like his bride; it always functioned, while the smaller sets, which were assigned to the individual troops hardly ever functioned.

At 1 p. m., the radio set was switched to the BBC news from London, and we heard the momentous announcement that Paris had been liberated that morning. The Marines shouted, "Who cares about Paris? What about Pont L'Eveque?"

Shortly thereafter, the town went up in flames all around us: the Germans had left delayed-action incendiary devices in houses from which the inhabitants had been driven out. I raced upstairs in the house in which we had taken cover and found one of these devices in a bedroom. It had not gone off and I managed to throw it into an empty courtyard.

We were ordered to withdraw and return to the 41 R. M. Commando main position on the mountain range. As I said before, there was only one Troop of 41 Commando in the town itself. I decided to risk taking the sunken road along which we had come by jeep that morning; it was the shortest way and I felt I could dodge the high trajectory German artillery fire. I would be able to hear the firing of these guns before the shells arrived. But now a good part of the town population was also leaving the town, I said to myself, "Das kann ja nicht gut gehen," (This is going to be a disaster). Then a shell was coming at us. I had not heard the firing of the gun. I realized that if the shell hit the road, I had no chance at all. I had to hope that it would hit the higher embankment. My luck held: the shell hit the embankment and not the road.

All along the roads from the Seine to Normandy beachhead, the Germans had forced their slave labor to dig air raid ditches, slit trenches about 6 feet long, 2 feet wide, 4 feet deep. These ditches provided cover to the drivers of German convoys when they were attacked by Allied aircraft. I was looking for such a ditch while the first shell was coming down. When I saw one, I grabbed two little girls about ten years old, and threw them into the ditch before I threw myself on top of them, just in time before the second shell hit. Now I carefully listened to the rapport from the firing of these high trajectory artillery guns, and when there was no indication of firing, I grabbed the girls and we made our way up the road to the next ditch. Of course, the girls got badly bruised (I was also carrying a Tommy gun) and they cried bitterly, but eventually we reached the farm where our First Aid station had been set up the night before, and I delivered the girls to our doctor. I never had a chance to look back and see what happened to other people on the road; hopefully they were following my example.

Sadly, none of us spoke French sufficiently to explain to these children that this traumatic experience was an unavoidable part of saving their lives. I could not stay in the First Aid Station. I had to go to our headquarters and tell the staff that I had returned.

Inevitably, as soon as it got dark we were on the move again: bypass Pont L'Eveque, going cross-country, without using any roads. It was tiring, but very successful. In the morning, we arrived in Beuzeville, where people received us with delicious fruits in the richest sour cream I had ever tasted. There were no such luxuries in wartime Great Britain, and even before the war I had been too poor to afford such treats.

Just as we were beginning to relax, a Frenchman came into the house which had been chosen as out headquarters and excitedly reported that there was a German gun position only 400 meters away. I reported that to Colonel Palmer, who was practically falling asleep and pouring down strong drinks. He just said "Take it in a hurry."

I managed to find one Bren gun crew and about six other Marines who were sufficiently awake to take part in one more attack. The Frenchman led us via some well-covered footpaths to an open meadow surrounded by the inevitable hedgerows. We peeped though one of theses hedgerows and saw the muzzle of an antitank gun.

It was pointed about 45 degrees away from us. I told the machine gun crew to stay behind and fire only if we got into trouble. I also told the Frenchman to stay put. No use to do an assault with people who were not trained for it.

We ran across the field as silently as we could. I headed straight for the gun and jumped through and over the hedgerow, which was hiding it. On the other side I was received by an aristocratic looking, tall Frenchman dressed in gray flannel trousers, blue-mauve blazer, striped shirt, no tie, but an elegant silk scarf. In perfect English he said, "Good morning gentlemen, you have been a long time coming." I said, "Good morning, where are the Germans?" "They left during the night after dismantling this gun."

This was the end of the Pont L'Eveque stage of our advance. A few days later, when we had an evening off, a few of us went back into Pont L'Eveque by jeep; once the roads were clear it was easy to travel in an hour or so the distances which we had had so laboriously covered in our night attacks. The town was back in full swing:

bars were open, there was music, singing and a bustle of activity.

## Across the Seine

We were drawn into one more very fierce engagement before we crossed the Seine. We were supposed to take over the lead of an attack from a British infantry battalion one midmorning, but when we caught up with those troops their advance had been halted. It was easy to see what had happened to them. They had advanced along a little road in the "classical" (stupid) fashion: two men leading a troop by about 50 yards. The Germans had let the two men come very close and held their fire until the whole troop was in sight. The resulting casualties were severe. I crawled into a spot from which I could see a good part of the road. There was no way to get at the dead or injured; the least little movement on our side drew very heavy machine gun fire.

As usual, we were ordered to get far away from the road in order to outflank the German rearguard. It took some time before we were in position for an assault, which was pretty much parallel to the road. Once more, it was Captain Stevens leading A Troop, who was ahead of us all. Halfway across the field I saw German soldiers moving in our direction. My first thought was that they were in an assault on us. Instinctively, I had the right reaction: I fired my Tommy gun while simultaneously throwing myself down, landing on my elbows and on my stomach. Once on the ground, I could take more deliberate aim at anything that moved. The exchange of machinegun and Tommy gun fire lasted only a short while. At that point Captain Stevens moved forward, and the Germans had withdrawn. Probably the moves we had observed were their attempt to prevent us outflanking them. On second thoughts, I doubted that they had intended to launch an attack on us.

We did not advance much further. Other Troops of 41 Commando were harassing the Germans across other fields. As usual, we waited till dark for the inevitable cross-country night march.

It might surprise "those skilled in the art" that neither we nor the infantry battalion which had proceeded us were able to call on artillery support. This German rearguard presented an ideal target for artillery, since we knew its exact location. With the benefit of hindsight, I assume that the British Army artillery was concentrated further south for the main army crossing of the Seine. Eventually, the British Army rapidly advanced from there to Brussels in just a few days.

The night march landed us on an estate about 10 miles from Deauville. And we were told that for the first time since D-Day we were out of range of German artillery and that we were going to get a few days of rest. The days were spent attending to our weapons and training reinforcements who had come from Great Britain to replace our casualties. In the evenings, "liberty" trucks would take us into Deauville, but on the first evening four of us went by jeep back to Pont L'Eveque, as I mentioned before.

The second evening, I joined the crowd which went into Deauville. Most of the Marines jumped off the truck before we got into the center of the town; they had discovered a bordello the night before and started to line up in front of it. Three sergeants and I found a wonderful, second floor restaurant and we had a sumptuous French meal totally unavailable in war-time Great Britain.

The next day and night it rained. There were not enough houses or barns to provide roofs for the whole Commando. We were miserable in makeshift tents or sleeping packed like sardines in the available buildings.

The following day, Colonel Palmer came around and in his quiet manner told us that we were ordered to advance to the Seine. He said, "Supposedly, the road is clear and there will be no resistance, but that's what we were promised a few days ago, when we took over from the infantry battalion. We'll proceed with caution."

We set off in jeeps and on foot, advancing cross-country whenever we thought we might walk into a trap. When, according to the maps, we were pretty close to the river, we were met by some well-armed French civilians. In all the months we had been in France, this was the first time we had met the armed underground. The French assured us that the road to the river was clear and that they would get us across at a village called Duclair.

When we got to the river, a large raft which could be pulled along a strong cable anchored on both sides of the Seine was waiting for us. Its buoyancy was just adequate to allow ferrying one jeep and about ten of us. Since, with my inadequate French, I was doing most of the talking, I was on the first jeep that was brought across. (Again I was not at all conscious of the historic significance of the occasion -too many tactical details to take care of.) After all, this was probably the most northerly crossing of the Seine by the Allied Armies, well inside the territory which had been prepared by the Germans for in depth defense.

We waited until two more jeeps had been ferried across before we drove into the nearest town (Barentin). We met more armed French civilians assuring us that there would be no surprises, and we rolled into town. This was the first undamaged town into which we had come, and the reception was wild. It was late afternoon; the whole population was on the streets. We slowly made our way to the center of the town, complete with market place and a picturesque Town Hall. To endless cheering, Colonel Palmer appeared on the balcony of the Town Hall together with the leaders of the French underground. The French were bringing in German prisoners, supposedly they had shot two of them claiming that they were hidden Gestapo men. Since they were treating all the other German prisoners decently, I felt that they knew what they were doing. In any case, we had strict orders not to interfere in the affairs of the population. I went into the Town Hall to take care of about 25 other German prisoners, mainly to calm them down. We had a very relaxed talk about their rearguard actions, where they were left without adequate support or supplies.

More Troops of 41 Commando were arriving, but before it got dark, we had to move on and take up positions beyond the town to prevent a potential German counterattack. Le Havre, the nearest big town, was still in German hands. That is the lot of the front-line troops: you can never enjoy the fruits of your successes. There was plenty of grumbling by the Marines that night!

The next morning we started a new (for us) type of warfare: from now on we mainly moved by jeep and truck.

## To Belgium

Having crossed the Seine and liberated, Barentin our tactics once more changed drastically: relying on information on German troop location provided by the French underground, we now did not hesitate to rapidly advance at maximum speed by jeep and truck, stopping only to pick up German prisoners, or to gather more information, or to be celebrated by the population of the towns and villages which we had liberated.

After two days of such "excursions" in the direction of the Belgium frontier, we were ordered back to participate in the assault on Le Havre. Once we reached the far outskirts of the town, we deployed off the roads into orchards and gardens, constantly moving on foot in the direction of the town center, which we reached that evening. We never saw any Germans; they had withdrawn into the town center before the assault and surrendered to the first Canadian troops who arrived there.

This was followed by the "siege" of Dunkirk, a few hundred Commandos with mobile guns besieging about 20,000 Germans. On one of our "trips" into Dunkirk we were almost caught and had to hide in the sewers to escape.

It took me two days to clean my clothing and recover from the nausea.

That German garrison stayed in Dunkirk until the end of the war, but a week after the sewer incident we moved on by truck for an assault on Ostend, whose outskirts we reached after one more move on foot by night. I remember that was the night of Yom Kippur, and we finished the night move in a nunnery.

Again, Ostend fell without a fight and we were ordered to a coastal town east of Ostend, Le Coq.

Western Europe

**Map of Normandy, north Western France, Belgium, South Holland, and South East England.**

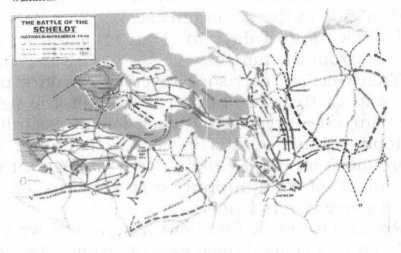

## Map of the Battle of the Scheldt"

# WALCHEREN

We stayed in LeCoq (De Haan, in Flemish) for about three weeks. Sometime during that time I was promoted to Sergeant. I did not care very much about it, except that it meant a little more pay into my bank account in Manchester. I never drew any pay from D-Day until I was discharged from the army in August 1946. I lived on the proceeds of loot confiscated from the Germans, particularly fancy German pistols, which could be sold for as much as £30. I knew that if I survived, I would want to go to go to a University to get a degree in Engineering, and I would need every penny I could save.

Also during that time, to my delight, Maurice Latimer from Three Troop, who had been injured in Normandy, returned to 41 R. M. Commando, so that I was not totally alone anymore. Sgt. Major O'Neill had returned to England soon after we broke out of the Normandy beachhead. Initially, I did not even know that he had left. That left me as the sole "mystery expert" from Three Troop during the fighting at Pont l'Eveque, the repeated night attacks which finally led us to the crossing of the Seine, the attack on Le Havre, the siege of Dunkirk, and the night move on to Ostend. Since the troops were more confident when I was along in any action, I was kept busy.

The harbor of Antwerp had fallen into Allied hands intact; its equipment had not been blown up, but it was inaccessible to Allied shipping, because both banks of the river Schelde, which leads into the harbor, were still held by the Germans. The south bank, German-held territory became known as the "Breskens Pocket", and the north bank was blocked by the heavily fortified island of Walcheren.

Then, in October, the Allied Air forces blew a major break into the dam at Westkapelle on Walcheren. A subsequent storm widened the gap and flooded the whole island, except for the rim of dunes around it.

While in Le Coq, I occasionally took a ride with an armored car troop, who went out to the flatlands of the Breskens Pocket to shoot up German positions. Once I was asked to go to a prisoner-of-war camp near Bruges to interview some prisoners who had been taken from the Bresken Pocket. Bunch of fanatics; couldn't get anything from them. They still believed that Der Fuehrer would eventually lead them to victory. "Wenn alle aushalten, dann muss gesiegt werden." (When everybody stands his man, victory is bound to follow) This was a stark reminder that the final stages of the war would not be a "walk-over".

During the last few days of October, we were briefed on our impending invasion of the island of

Walcheren. We had learned our lesson on the D-Day Normandy beaches: maps provided by British Intelligence showing every German fortification, artillery and antitank gun position had to be studied carefully to adapt tactics to deal with them without excessive casualties. These maps showed a considerably denser degree of fortifications than we had encountered in Normandy, but the island was "sunk"; except for the rim of dunes around it, where the German fortifications were located, the island was flooded. There would be no fast communication with vehicles between these fortifications; they could hardly reinforce each other.

On the late evening of October 31st, we embarked once more. It was D-Day all over again: in the dark a large flotilla of ships assembled to sail into the North Sea with the aim of landing right at the broken dam at Westkapelle on Walcheren. The morning once more found us in the company of destroyers, cruisers and battleships which were dueling with the German shore guns, but the gun battles seemed more intense than what we had experienced on D-Day.

The sea was rough. There was a hauling wind, but we were on LSTs (Landing Ship Tank), not the much lighter LSI (Landing Ship Infantry) on which we had been on D-Day. Each LST held about four tanks and one or two Marine Commando Troops, so that, in spite of the rough sea and the flat bottom of the LST, we were not tossed around unduly. Also, we had a much better view of our surroundings than we had had on D-Day. Morale was high: in all ranks there were officers, warrant officers and marines who had survived D-Day, the hedgerow war in Normandy, ten night attacks which brought us to the Seine, the siege of Dunkirk and our march to Ostend. We were battle-hardened and very experienced.

At Westkapelle, the dam and the beach run from northeast to southwest. 41 R. M. Commando was to land at the northeast tip of the dam, to make its way east to the major gun positions at Domburg, while 47 and 48 R. M. Commandos were to land on the southwest end of the dam, to make their way south towards Flushing. 41 Commando's landing spot was only about 300 yards away from the German gun positions at Westkapelle.

There comes a moment in each of these sea-borne invasions when the landing crafts have to go ahead alone, while the destroyers and battleships, which have a deeper draw, have to stay behind. At that critical moment, the navy laid down a dense smoke screen for us to cover the landing beach and blind the German gunners, who were only a few hundred yards away from our intended landing spot at Westkapelle and its broken dam.

It didn't help us very much; the wind was too strong and the smoke screen was blown away too soon. Now the German guns, which had been battling with the destroyers, were turning around and were being depressed to fire at us point blank. At that moment, a British rocket ship beached itself in front of the German gun positions and fired its rockets, point blank, into the slots of the concrete German fortifications. That gave us our chance to land.

As on D-Day, I jumped off the landing ship as soon as I felt the waters were shallow enough to wade, and I rushed up the beach and off the beach into Westkapelle. This time, the whole Commando did the same, nobody, got "beach happy", so we had almost no casualties, unlike on D-Day where we lost half the Commando.

The beach was full of mines which had been washed out of the dunes. It was unlikely that they were still functioning. We took no notice of them. We rushed up the beach into the boulders of the broken dam, excellent cover against the German machine guns. But we couldn't stay; we had to get on. Westkapellle was a lunar landscape, not a single house habitable. What had not been destroyed by the air force bombardment was ruined by the subsequent flood. Not a soul living in that place anymore. We assembled and disappeared amongst the ruined houses.

German artillery fire was heavily concentrated on the 47/48 R. M. landing spot (I believe this is where 3 Troop's Hamilton was killed), but apart from sporadic machine gun fire, nobody seemed to take much notice of us.

At the end of the main street of Westkapelle was a light tower which afforded an overview of the whole area and which was marked on our maps as an artillery observation post. We had hoped that one of our tanks could be used to fire its canon into the light tower, but none of the tanks had made it up from the beach as yet. The situation was intolerable; the fire on the 47/48 R. M. Commando landing spot was just too accurate, so I decided to end it all. I walked down the middle of the Westkapelle main street, with my Tommy gun pointing down, shouting, "Kommen Sie heraus und ergeben Sie sich, bevor unsere Panzer Geschuetze eingesetzt warden." (Come out and surrender before our tanks go into action)

It worked; out came a very cocky German sergeant, who told me that he would only surrender under "conditions." He had been taken prisoner before, in the invasion of Norway and he had been mistreated by the Norwegians. I carefully listened to his "conditions". His back was towards the tower, and I made sure that he would not see the row of broken houses on the left of the main street, because Maurice Latimer was stealthily making his way through those houses into the tower.

It wasn't long before Maurice had led out the whole crew, making them, too, disappear into the shattered houses. The sergeant didn't see any of this, but when Maurice and his prisoners had disappeared, I said to the Sergeant. "O. K, the game is up, your crew has surrendered. I cannot accept "conditions". Let's go to the Prisoner Collection point. If you try to give hell to your crew for surrendering, you'll be shot." The picture of Maurice marching the prisoners towards the beach was taken at that time.

And then came the floods. We had been warned of the exact time of high tide (about 11 a. m.) and that we would have to scramble to the upper floors or even the roofs of the shattered houses. We just had not believed that the tide would come so suddenly, so most of us got soaked for the second time that day. I found a good place, just below a partially broken roof, where I could keep dry and observe the dunes towards Domburg. We all wondered why we were not being fired at by the Germans, who were no more than 300 yards away.

Two hours later, the floods receded as fast as they had come. Now it was time to make our way east toward Domburg, but there was only one connection between Westkapelle and the German strongpoint whose guns had swung around to fire at us before the British Navy rocket launcher had fired its rockets straight into the gun slots. That connection was the causeway, an extension of the broken dam. Surely it would be heavily defended. Mortars and machine guns were readied to provide cover for us to run along the causeway into the German position, but we used our favorite tactic: just run in without covering fire and take everyone by surprise. Covering fire alerts the enemy that an attack is coming.

I believe there was some firing on both sides, and we had some casualties (we lost 11 men that whole day), but when we got into the strongpoint we were faced with an incredible spectacle: the German crews were physically and mentally shattered. Their hands were shaking uncontrollably, and they could hardly walk. The naval bombardment, followed by rockets exploding inside their concrete fortifications had sent them into shell shock. That was the reason we had not been bothered by machine gun fire while hiding in the shattered houses, and that was the reason for the erratic defense of the causeway.

Were these shattered people happy to talk to me! No time to waste, "Show me an unmined path into the next strongpoint." Readily done. We sent the Germans back towards the landing beach while we moved forward. Unbelievably, at the next strongpoint we were met by two well-dressed German officers, who were only too keen to surrender. They came out with their whole crew. We couldn't even spare guards for them; we just told them to march west while we marched east.

It was a similar story at the next strongpoint, and that advance carried us to the edge of the extensive minefields around the Domburg long-range gun positions. Apart from the guns in and around Flushing, the Domburg guns were the only guns which could still interfere with Allied shipping sailing into the harbor of Antwerp. Now we got ambitious: take this formidable fortress tonight. Keep up the surprise.

As we started to pick our way across the minefields, four Hurricane fighters appeared in the sky. They flew from west to east parallel to our advance, but they were flying more inland over the flooded area, thereby minimizing the risk of German anti-aircraft fire. As they caught up with us, the first fighter took a sharp turn left and made his run onto the strongpoint. Machine guns blazing, he dropped his bomb well into the strongpoint. The next fighter plane dropped his bomb closer to us. The bomb of the third plane almost came to the far edge of the minefield. All this time, we kept going. Then the fourth plane made his run almost on top of us, but he didn't drop his bomb! (Two weeks later some of the 41st R. M. Commando officers met these fighter pilots in Brussels. They explained that they knew exactly where we were, because they saw our green berets against the white sand of the dunes.)

We had made maximum use of this magnificent cover. We now were inside the Domburg battery, but it was getting dark. I felt sure that the battery crew had no idea of our presence; all I needed was a few Germans to persuade everybody else to surrender. While X Troop of 41st Commando was systematically taking up a position just at the edge of the strongpoint, I went right inside to look for possible prisoners. It was obvious that the Germans were still taking cover inside their bunkers, expecting more air attacks or further shelling from the British battleships. Finally, I saw a German soldier standing quite leisurely at the entrance of one of the bunkers. I said calmly, "Ergeben Sie sich." (Surrender) He did nothing of the sort: he dove back into the bunker. I tried to fire my Tommy gun, but it jammed. Within a second some hand grenades were thrown at me, or at the spot where I had been, I had already taken cover in the sand. I got a splinter in my cheek, which is there to this day. When I sensed that there were no more grenades in the air, I dove into another bunker. It was occupied by three Austrians, who surrendered readily. I waited until it was dark. There now was sporadic machinegun and rifle fire from both sides, but I was sure I could get out in the dark. I left the Austrians in the bunker, and it wasn't long before I reemerged in the X Troop position. Neither they nor the Germans had noticed me. (Next morning I learned that the Major in Charge of X Troop had gone out to look for me after he noticed that I was in trouble. He was killed in the rifle and machinegun fire which I had heard. That death was hard to take: the Major was married and had two children.)

X Troop was left to hold down the Domburg battery. One other Troop and the Headquarters Troop, to which I belonged and which included Colonel Palmer, Major Woods and the Adjutant, moved out towards the Westkapelle - Domburg road to bypass the strongpoint and get into Domburg. It was now pitch dark and we felt safe to make our way along the road.

Domburg that night was the most gruesome sight I ever saw in my life (to this day, as it says in the Bible). Several houses and the church were burning. The streets were littered with men, women and children in those beautiful local costumes, who had been hit by our naval gunfire dueling with the German strongpoint outside the village. I could just imagine it: when in the morning the naval bombardment started, they had run out to get a view of the ocean, and when they saw the landing force, they had gone out into the streets to celebrate their impending liberation, not realizing how inaccurate these artillery bombardments can be. Now, as we moved in to really liberate them, it was pitch dark, the burning houses providing the only illumination. The town was overcrowded with all the people from nearby villages which had been flooded. There was literally blood flowing in the streets.

B Troop of 41st Commando silently moved through the town to take up positions just outside a German strongpoint at the other (east) end of the town. X Troop was still besieging the Domburg batteries. The Germans had no idea that we were "in town"; they came into town to visit their girlfriends and we grabbed them. That is the advantage of moving silently and firing weapons only when there is an absolute need. Some German soldiers even came from the Domburg battery. They must have thought that after they lost sight of me and had killed the Major, they had repelled our attack. We set up a prisoner-of-War post on the second floor of a house opposite the house which we had chosen as the Commando headquarters. Some Dutch men appeared with pistols and rifles, and I commandeered them to guard the prisoners by watching the stairs leading up to that second floor and watching the windows to avoid anyone jumping out. We could just spare one Marine to be in charge of the "POW post". Since I was the only one who spoke Dutch, I was in big demand. I doubt that there were more than two or three people in Domburg who spoke English, unlike what one would find now. Maurice Latimer was with B Troop.

Now that we were in town, the Dutch were convinced that there would be no more naval shelling, so they started to move the dead and the blood from the streets.

Four of us moved into a house diagonally opposite our headquarters. Two older women and two young girls sat around a table illuminated by just one candle. We struck up a conversation with them. The girls made no bones about it that they had German soldier boyfriends. I knew enough about Dutch girls to realize that they were not prostitutes. Young girls will be young girls, and there were plenty of ordinary young men amongst the German army.

I was near total exhaustion. We had not slept at all the previous night, when we were sailing on the landing ship. We had been soaked twice, and I had been injured, but had not lost much blood. I was absolutely set on getting a good night's sleep. A tiny staircase wound up to a small bedroom under the roof. I put a table across the top of the winding staircase; nobody would be able to come up without making a lot of noise. It all worked out fine; I got a few hours of very good sleep.

## Second Day

It was bright daylight by the time I walked across the street into our headquarters. The Domburg battery had surrendered when its gunners noticed that X Troop was right inside their gun positions and that we had taken Domburg. (They didn't realize that there were probably less than a hundred of us in the town.) Snipers from the strongpoint at the other end of the town were giving us a lot of trouble; we had to walk carefully through the town. We also learned that of the 28 tanks which were supposed to support the Westkapelle invasion force, only two had made it ashore.

Additional 41R. M. Commando Troops were arriving. I was talking to one of their officers at the entrance of our headquarters when he suddenly threw himself on me, dragging me inside, "There is a German soldier at the window right opposite us." I had to explain to him that the second floor of that house was our temporary POW camp. A more serious disaster was avoided just in time, when one of our two tanks rumbled into town, saw the Germans at the window and was about to fire at them.

Young Dutch boys with pistols and rifles were dragging out the two Dutch girls whom we had met the night before and proceeded to cut their hair. I told the boys that if they were such heroes they should take care of the German snipers who were bothering us. But our Adjutant warned me, "No interference in civilian affairs." That was the Allied policy.

No Allied food rations ever reached us on this or subsequent days on Walcheren. Some British papers reported that rations were dropped to us by parachute. We never saw them, nor did we need them: the German fortifications were loaded with good food, including fresh eggs, flour, live chickens, which we had not seen for months. We took our share before handing these supplies to the Dutch.

In the afternoon, we were told to turn around and go back to Westkapelle to help 48 and 47 R. M. Commando in their push to Flushing. We left one Troop of 41 R. M. Commando and our "superior" armored forces (that's how I saw it described in a German diary a few days later) of two tanks to prevent the Germans from re-taking Domburg.

We reached Westkapelle just in time to find quarters safe from the inevitable floods. The night was clear and cold, and from our elevated quarters we had the most impressive view of the V2 Rockets going up from the Dutch coast to the north of us, on their way to London. This was Hitler's "weapon against which there would be no defense"; we had read all about it in the British newspapers. In the middle of the night "they" reserved one of these V2s for us. It landed somewhere near the beach where we had landed the previous day. I doubt it did any harm.

## Third Day

At dawn, we marched off at a furious pace south towards Flushing to catch up with 47/48 Commando. We took some German prisoners, who could not keep up with our pace, so we commandeered a Dutch farmer and his horse drawn wagon, and the Germans rode while we marched.

In the afternoon, word came through that 47 and 48 Commando had linked up with 4 Commando in Flushing and that we were to turn around and get back to Domburg.

We dropped the Germans off at the POW collection point in Westkapelle, and we got back to Domburg that evening. A school had been commandeered as our headquarters. The one Troop we had left behind, helped by our "superior armored forces", which we used only as mobile guns, had taken the German strongpoint just to the east of Domburg, so that at least we were not bothered by snipers any more while walking in the town.

Prisoners I interviewed that night confirmed what we already knew from our maps: that the next strongpoint was well armed and manned by dedicated Luftwaffe ground personnel.

## Fourth Day

For this day, 41st Commando was put under the command of the colonel of 1OIA Commando and his 2nd in command, because the Norwegian troop of the Inter Allied Commando was now with us. We had learned that the area between the Luftwaffe strongpoint (let's call it W19, though I am not sure that the number is correct) and the flooded part of the country was defended by a German battalion which had been brought up from the Russian front. Thus we were out of "tricks"; the next move had to be a frontal attack.

I didn't like the way our temporary commanders prepared for this. They were amateurs. Maurice Latimer came to the same conclusion. Though we were right up in the front line, we found ourselves a relatively safe place to observe events, but absolutely set on NOT moving.

When one of our Troops started to move (practically without any preparatory fire or even any intensive covering fire), the Germans opened up with everything they had, including massive volleys of ground-to-ground rockets, which we had never before experienced.

In his quiet, calm and friendly way, 41st R. M. Commander, Colonel Palmer, who was right there with us, persuaded everyone to call off this attack. "Sorry things went so badly; we'll try something else tomorrow."

We of the headquarter Troop went all the way back to Domburg to the school building which was our headquarters. There were no new prisoners, so I had the night off.

## Fifth Day

By about noon next day we were back on the edge of the Luftwaffe strongpoint. We had discovered a small, concrete dugout which afforded a view over most of the area ahead of us. Colonel Palmer, Major Woods, our faithful signaler, who never carried a weapon but cherished his huge signaling set as if it were his bride, and a few others were in and out of this concrete dugout. Major Woods (he was a former civilian, while Palmer and the Adjutant were professionals) had brought pencil and paper and drew up what we now would call a spreadsheet, specifying exact times, targets for all the weapons we could bring to bear and the time of movement for each attacking Troop. I had read about this type of planning, I had heard a lecture about it, but I had never seen it done in practice.

The officers in charge of our two tanks were brought in to show them where they would fit into the plan. They were NOT to charge ahead of us, but were to be used as mobile guns only. The Sherman Tank was to stay in the dunes at a high spot not too far from our lookout point; the converted Bren carrier was to follow the Troops which were assigned to advance into the woods outside the strongpoint. Each Troop commander was given exact instructions when and where to fire with which weapon. The most impressive part to me was that Palmer and Woods never gave orders; they had their own way of quietly convincing everyone in a most friendly way.

In the middle of the afternoon our friends, the Hurricane bombers came in. Again, they flew from the west to east over the flooded areas so as to avoid German anti-aircraft fire. Again, they peeled off to make their bombing and strafing runs, but this time they had been assigned targets to fit in with the overall plan.

Our firing plan for 3-inch mortars, machineguns and tank went into action. At the last moment, before everyone was to move forward, a slight mistake was discovered in the timetable for the Troop which was closest to the ocean, and I was sent to warn them to delay. To get there fast I had to expose myself to the strongpoint, but I was pretty confident that after the aerial attack, followed by our covering fire, the German gunners still had their heads down. Just as I reached the Troop, three very heavily dressed German soldiers came running out of the strongpoint, into one of our Troop's positions at an incredible speed. They reached the Troop at the same time I did. Totally out of breath, they threw themselves onto the sand. After I had given my message to the Troop commander, I turned to the Germans to find out why they had come out without a white flag, running at such speed. Still out of breath they declared, "Gesund in die Gefangenschaft das ist unser Ziel." (become a prisoner of war in a healthy state, that is our aim) They were not afraid to be fired on by us, but they expected to be shot in the back by the Luftwaffe fanatics.

Amazingly, with our moving covering fire, the Germans were still surprised to suddenly find us inside their strongpoint. Some of the marines moved right through the maze of bunkers without bothering to accept surrenders. I wasted too much time looking for high-ranking officers. When I found two of them, they turned out to be nasty and uncooperative, but their troops surrendered readily without their orders.

We were at the northern part of the strongpoint, the part that was closest to the sea. Y Troop of 41st Commando was at the southern part. They too went right through the strongpoint without accepting surrender. At the end of the strongpoint, the Captain of Y Troop and his batman sat down on a slight elevation. Supposedly the Captain said, "This is as far as we will go today," but then both he and his batman were shot in the back from one of the bypassed bunkers. They were both killed.

Y Troop had two of what I called "the survivor sergeants," highly experienced men. They had NOT displayed themselves openly, but they knew from which bunker the shots which killed the captain had been fired. Giving each other covering fire, they proceeded to throw hand grenades into all nearby bunkers. Even when the Germans came out with a white flag, they fired at some who were behaving suspiciously.

I did not witness all that. I record it here only because I felt both these deaths as a personal loss. The Captain had joined us only during our hedgerow war in Normandy and had volunteered to go out with me on one of our night patrols, almost the first night he was with 41st Commando. He was a small, slim, very fit man, maybe two years older than I, who always carried a rifle. He chided us for using Tommy guns: his rifle had a longer range and was more accurate than our Tommy guns. On this, his first patrol, we heard a noise from what I deemed to be a German patrol coming toward us. I had been in that situation before, so I fired my Tommy gun, but there really was no target for his rifle. Ever after, our good-natured argument about rifles and Tommy guns continued whenever we ran into each other.

His batman's name was Moses, but he was Welsh, not Jewish. He knew Aberdovey, the picturesque town in Wales which had been the birthplace of Three Troop. Now, one of the benefits of being with British troops in the "field" is the occasional movie shows of Hollywood or British films in tents or requisitioned movie theaters. British soldiers heckle these movies continuously; the "cornier" the film, the better the heckling. The total absence of members of the opposite sex makes the heckling still more spicy. Moses was the absolute master of such heckling.

Back to our "set piece" attack. Outside the Luftwaffe strongpoint, the attack supported by the converted Bren gun carrier had gone well, but the carrier following the troops ran across a mine and lost one of its tracks. That was the end of 50% of our "armored support".

Once again we had hundreds of prisoners. We had to get them back to our collection point in Domburg before it got dark. I kept my eyes on the "nasties" from the Luftwaffe, one of whom had the gall to taunt me. "Aber was aus dem Russen wird das wisst Ihr noch nicht." (You have no idea how to handle the Russians)

Back in our headquarters, I set up for a massive interrogation of the prisoners. All those who invoked the Geneva Convention, that they only had to give their name and serial number, were immediately dismissed. I didn't need them; there were enough who were willing to talk. My aim was to find out how much resistance we would meet in the next strongpoint, and what was the quality of the battalion which had just come from the Russian front to guard the areas outside the strongpoints.

I came to the conclusion that there was nothing special about the next strongpoint; its crews had been changed frequently, and I got a very clear picture of the "battalion" from the Russian front. Amongst the prisoners was a German Captain from that battalion. He reminded me so much of my favorite mathematics teacher back in my high school in Germany that I had an instant rapport with him. The battalion was a myth; apart from his company, which had surrendered with him, there was little else. He had a very low opinion of the Luftwaffe officers who had given us so much trouble. "They dodged the whole war. Until you attacked yesterday, they never heard a shot fired in earnest." I said, "What are you going to do with these types after the war?" He shrugged his shoulders and I said, "Unless people like you stand up against them, there will just be endless trouble, even after the war." Of course, what I really meant was that he had to stand up against these devoted Nazis right now in the POW camp. I hope he got the point.

It was shortly after ten when I felt I had enough information.

## Sixth Day

Before dawn next morning, we were back at our "front," the end of the Luftwaffe strongpoint, where we had lost the Y Troop Captain and his batman the evening before. We were back at our old tricks of silently picking our way across a minefield, without covering or supporting fire.

Once just inside the strongpoint, we came across two rather small German soldiers dressed in badly fitting, long overcoats, "schlepping" a huge canister of coffee. I told them to take me to the Captain in charge of the strongpoint, but they rolled in the sand and cried that they would be regarded as traitors even in a POW camp. We had to desist from our order; these men were incapable of moving, literally scared stiff, not of us, but of their own superiors.

The dawn was gray and dark. We went further into the strongpoint. Suddenly, a figure emerged from a bunker, shouting, "Verflixed nochmal, wo ist denn mein Kaffee?" (damn it all, where is my coffee) A split- second hesitation: was I going to walk up to this officer quietly, or was I going to rush him? At that moment, a figure which I recognized as Maurice Latimer was literally flying through the air, pulling down the officer with what in rugby we call a high tackle, stubbing his face into the sand.

Maurice had come up with another troop. Hearing the German officer curse, he, too, realized that we had the man we were looking for. I was with Colonel Palmer and Major Woods. I just said; "Here is the guy we are looking for." Palmer walked up to the German Captain, saluted him, and in a very friendly way said, "Good morning, Sir, perhaps you would care to come around the strongpoint with us and order your troops to surrender." I translated that into as polite a German as I could muster. By now, Maurice, who hated German officers but had a lot of sympathy for the ordinary German soldiers, was menacingly pointing his Tommy gun at the Captain.

It wasn't long before everybody in the strongpoint had surrendered. Then we forced the Captain to walk with us to the remaining German headquarters, which was well outside the strongpoint. As we walked along a wooded path, we were met by a German colonel and a German major, who informed us that they had agreed that all remaining troops would surrender by eleven o'clock that morning. This information was confirmed by our faithful signaler. Apparently, there had been a surrender to No 4 Commando, which had come up from Flushing and was operating to the south of us.

We didn't hang around. We had more important things to do. We left the prisoners and the glorious surrender to others and marched off at our furious pace all the way back to Domburg, where we gouged ourselves on a terrific breakfast, which Ben, the Arab whom we had picked up on D-Day, had prepared, complete with eggs and pancakes, the latter made by me from German flour, butter and liqueur.

## Seventh Day and Beyond

In the morning, we buried our dead in a cemetery in Domburg, each body wrapped in a blanket. Some of the dead had been so severely wounded that the shape of the body was not recognizable through the tightly wrapped blankets. Though we had been witness to almost all the action, we were still pretty shaken.

In the afternoon, the whole of 41st R. M. Commando gathered in a little movie house in Domburg. There were so many marines in the balcony seats that I was worried that the balcony might collapse. Palmer reviewed all the events of the past six days and thanked the various units and Troops for specific actions.

A few days later, we returned to Le Coq by truck, boat and marching via Flushing. While crossing the Schelde we saw the fruits of our labor: Allied mine sweepers clearing the Schelde entrance to the harbor of Antwerp.

At about that time, Colonel Palmer called me into his office and, in the presence of Major Woods only, said to me, "I am going to put you in for a commission in the field (promotion to an officer), but tell me who you really are." I was surprised they did not know. I said, "I am German; I was educated as an orthodox Jew. My grandfather came from Holland to marry my grandmother. We lived in a little town near the Dutch frontier, and that is why I speak Dutch."

In turn, we were given two days "leave" to go to Brussels. Before the landing in Walcheren, I had, by chance, once met Hamilton (Reich) from Three Troop. He vaguely described to me the location of a Jewish café which he had discovered.

In Brussels I miraculously found the café easily. This was the first time I met Jewish civilians since having been on leave in London well before D-Day. Soon a young woman came in and showed me a picture of Hamilton, asking me whether I knew him, since I wore the same green beret and parachutist wings. I had to give her the sad news that Hamilton had been killed in the invasion of Walcheren.

When I returned to Le Coq, my best friend from Three Troop, Andrew Kershaw, who had gone to an Officers Training School just before D-Day, had joined 41st R. M. Commando.

## After Glow

We returned to Walcheren two weeks later. This time we came by land and were initially quartered in the first village beyond the causeway which leads to South Beveland (Nieuwland). It was now very cold. I became friendly with a Dutch family who had two daughters, 14 and 16 years old. The girls found Dutch skates for me and we regularly went skating on the "grachten" (canals) at night. They both had boyfriends, so this relationship remained platonic, but the exhilaration of skating at great speeds over endless waterways took my mind totally off the war.

I became an officer on December 3rd, and I had to move into the Officers Mess. As I wrote to my friends through my cover address, the Wislickis in Manchester at the time, "and in Churchillian style, I can not help wondering how far I have come, going, in only four short years, from an enemy alien internment camp to being an officer in a British elite unit, without having gone to an Officers Training School."

The Mess was initially a distinct degradation of my standard of living, In the Commandos there are no cooks; groups form to take turns feeding each other. We had a very congenial group, mainly of survivor sergeants, and we put a lot of effort and initiative into organizing and cooking our food. In the Mess, Colonel Palmer did not care about food, and, to quote one of the officers, "you eat what the batmen leave over." Eventually we hired local civilians to cook for the Mess.

On and off, I was involved with Walcheren almost until the end of the war in Europe. I will record here only those happenings which bore on the fighting.

Several of the Troops of 41st Commando were stationed once more "up north" in the Westkapelle-Domburg area. From the center of Walcheren we had to go up north by amphibious vehicles, DWCs, a rough ride even in good weather. It must be remembered that the next island along the Dutch coast, Schouwen, remained in German hands until the end of the war. For the Allies it was not worthwhile to invade it, but we had to guard continuously against some crazy action from there. Gradually, our positions were taken over by the newly recruited Dutch Army. Being the only officer in the Brigade who spoke Dutch, I was frequently involved in this gradual take-over.

The Dutch started to rebuild the Westkapelle dam. They did it the old fashioned way, with mats, sticks, loam, clay and sand, using no mechanical equipment at all. Out of the blue, I was ordered by Brigade Headquarters to attend a high-powered conference on the rebuilding of the dam. A Colonel from our Brigade and a Colonel from the Royal Engineers came to fetch me for the meeting, which took place on the mainland. Two American generals participated in the meeting, as did about five civilians from Walcheren. The Americans offered to sink a string of flat bottomed tank landing crafts loaded with concrete to act as a breakwater behind which the dam could be rebuilt. The Dutch wouldn't hear of it. They said that they had built the dams their way for 450 years. I couldn't help telling them that therefore their methods were 450 years outdated.

A few weeks later, another storm severely damaged the newly built dam. Now the American offer was accepted and the rebuilding of a new dam could proceed safely.

Xmas 1944, the Battle of the Bulge, Hitler's last, crazy attempt to push back the Allied armies, was in full swing. Two one-man submarines were swept ashore in the Westkapelle-Domburg area. Their crew was rushed to my office in Middelburg to find out what was happening. One of the prisoners was a dedicated fanatic who wouldn't talk, but the other one was very cooperative: they had been sent out from Schouwen to make their way to the mouth of the Schelde and to torpedo Allied shipping going to Antwerp. We notified the British Navy immediately, and within an hour a Naval Intelligence officer joined us. They had expected this type of attack and were now happy to get confirmation. From our interrogation it was obvious that these one-man submariners knew very little about navigation; they had to follow the coastline. Now the navy knew where to concentrate their defense devices.

While I was in the eastern part of Walcheren, a picturesque town by the name of Veere, it was decided to evacuate with amphibious vehicles the civilian population from one of the islands that effectively was in the no-man's-land between us and Schouwen.

As the amphibious vehicles moved into the more open sea, German guns were shelling us. It is bad enough to be shelled while on a landing craft with highly experienced landing troops, but it is a most uncomfortable experience in a landing craft full of civilians dressed in the beautiful costumes of that area. Luckily, none of the German shells scored a hit.

That was the last action I saw on Walcheren.

In the summer of 1964, I was on an engineering assignment in Antwerp. My wife, Anita, and my children, Aviva and Dany, came to join me. One lovely weekend we drove to Westkapelle on Walcheren. There was now an impressive monument to commemorate our landing. I walked down the main street to the Light Tower as I had done 20 years earlier. All the houses had been rebuilt; the style had not at all been changed. Everything was so familiar and so peaceful. Anita was totally shaken when I described to her the ferocity of the ocean and hail of fire with which we had to deal in our landing. She sensed the war.

We drove to Domburg and first "hit" the beaches. They were incredibly beautiful: a new dyke with a causeway had been built between Walcheren and North Beveland, and a subsequent storm had deposited white sand all along these endless beaches. Concrete fortifications, and barbed wire had been removed. The dunes had been meticulously restored. The day was exceptionally hot, and literally thousands of Germans were taking in the sun and the sea. With the new Dutch and German super highways, Walcheren is now only 2 1/2 hours away from the gray and polluted Ruhr district, a drive which the Germans were only too willing to take just for a single day of sunshine at the ocean.

We went into Domburg. Near the church, which was burning when I first came to this town and which had been rebuilt just as it was before, a man a little bit older than I was selling fresh herring from his cart. We indulged ourselves. I said, "I came here on the evening of November 1st, 1944." He said, "You were one of the Tommies who landed at Westkapelle?" When I confirmed that, he said, "It's about time you guys come back and again drive out all these Moffen." (Dutch derogatory word for Germans)

P. S. Maurice Latimer (Moritz Levy) belonged to a socialist Sudeten German organization. In 1938, when the Germans marched into the Sudetenland after the betrayal at Munich, he held up the German army with one machine gun. Amazingly, he came out alive from this encounter. He was also in the Commando Dieppe raid in 1942.

Imperial War Museum

**Approaching Walcheren on November 1st 1944.
Each landing craft carried 4 tanks and 2 Commando
Troops (about 100 men).**

Imperial War Museum

## Smoke screen laid down by the British navy for the landing on Walcheren

Imperial War Museum

**Tank landing ship (LCT) on the beach of
Westkapelle. The ramps, which we had used to get
off the ship before it landed, are up. The hatch and
the short ramp, which allows the tanks to roll off,
are open**

Imperial War Museum

**A flail tank after leaving the LCT. Of the 28 tanks.
which were supposed to support us, only two made
it ashore. All other tanks including this flail tank did
not make it ashore. Flail tanks were used to
detonate mines in a mine field, thus creating a path
for troops and vehicles.... ...**

Imperial War Museum

## Looking back at he landing beach at Westkapelle

Imperial War Museum

**Marine Commandos on the main street (Zuidstraat)
of Westkapelle leading to the light tower used as a
German Army artillery observation post.**

Imperial War Museum

**Group on the right: Meeting of 4th Brigade officers on the street of Westkapelle. From left to right: Col. Hope, 2nd in Command 4th Brigade; Col. Palmer, OC 41 Royal Marine Commando, Major Franks, 2nd in Command 10 IA Commando; Brig. General "Jumbo" Leicester OC 4th Brigade; Major Peter Woods, 2nd in Command 41 Royal Marine Commando. Note the two amphibious carriers in the back**

Imperial War Museum

**Maurice Latimer marching German soldiers towards the prisoner collection point, after he and I persuaded the Germans to surrender. The lighthouse which they had manned is at the end of the street.**

Imperial War Museum

**German strong point in Westkapelle totally destroyed by rockets of the British Navy.**

Imperial War Museum

**The landscape on Walcheren after the island had been flooded as a result of the destruction of the dam at Westkapelle**

Imperial War Museum

**Gun in the German strong point in Domburg.**

WW2Museum.com

**Monument at Westkapelle for
commemorating our landing**

# Containing the German Army in Holland

41st Royal Marine Commando spent the rest of the war in southern Holland facing an aggressive, confident-from-the-Arnheim-battle German Army on flat, canal-interlaced territory. Fighting was now getting close to my former home. When the British and American paratroopers landed across the Rhine in March, 1944, I watched from a vantage point unaware that my cousin, from the same German hometown, now an American paratrooper, was among those who were participating in the final assault on the thousand- year Nazi empire.

A few days later, the Saturday before Easter, I took off and drove with Andrew Kershaw to the still-smoldering remains of my hometown, which had been conquered 36 hours before.

Last-minute fanatical resistance, inevitably answered by tactical fire and high explosive bombing before the British armored attack, ensured a flaming end of the Hitler ideology in this little town, pulling down with it the picturesque remnants of a thousand-year history, including the old synagogue with its Hebrew School, which had been the focal point of our youth. But our house, which had been Gestapo headquarters during the war, was fully intact. A detachment of British Field Security service was moving in to prepare for the arrival of Military Government staff.

We ran into Field Marshal Montgomery, who had made his temporary headquarters on one of the moated estates just outside the town.

# TEREZIN

Towards the end of the war I heard, via my uncle in New York, my brother Teo and my cover address, from people who had reached Switzerland in the Eichmann exchange of "Trucks for Jews" that my parents were still alive in Theresienstadt. When the war drew towards its end in early May, 1945, I set out with a driver and a jeep to find them.

The attached story was written in one night when I returned from that trip.

# EUROPE 1945 (written May 1945)

First Day. At last, we are ready to push off. The driver has only been told about the trip a quarter of an hour ago. He is all for it. Some people remark, "Lucky chap". I still have regrets that I couldn't take Sgt. A. along. He does everything I want done on his own initiative; there is no need for any orders. Still, can't be helped. The weather is perfect. We travel in shirt sleeves. The driver informs me that the brakes of the jeep don't work and I promise that we'll get that mended on the way. Leave GOES (South Beveland) round about 12 o' clock. Collect some papers at Brigade HQ. "All assistance is to be given..." etc., etc.

In ROSENDAAL two Canadians ask us for a lift. They are returning from BRUSSELS leave. "VE Day in B. have we had a time!!" It turns out they are going up to BREMEN so we decide to stick together till MUNSTER. In Tilburg we pull up for the repair of the brakes. The mechanic is very slow about the job. It takes an hour and a half. It's now terribly hot. I get quite impatient, but driving from there to NIJMEGEN cools me down a bit. Something is still wrong with the jeep, but I can't find out what.

CLEVE - EMMERICH - BOCHOLT, everywhere complete destruction. "Bob", the driver, who hasn't seen all this before just can't grasp it. The Canadians are cracking jokes, "There is a house still intact over there, bloody natives living in it; far too good for them." My maps are very small scale, they only show the towns, still I know the country around here – the roads are appallingly bad. BOCHOLT is hardly recognizable. Total destruction. I think of the lovely days I spent here before 1938. There is a canteen in a lovely house; the British soldiers are having their tea and cake in the garden. In the corner sits a nice girl. Everywhere else she would be besieged; here nobody bothers. Non-fraternization works very well during the daylight. Forward! I want to make MUNSTER tonight. Passing through BORKEN I go slow. The Allied Military Government is now in our former home. They have dressed the building up terrifically. It looks very impressive. I am glad. That'll teach the Jerries. With their belief in the mystic, they will not fail to notice the lesson.

Over the well-known road to MUNSTER. We come into the American sector; in every village there is a Yankee billet. The men sit outside their houses and feel bored. We stop at one group. "When are we going home?" they ask. "How are you getting on here?" "It's lousy during the day, but we do all right at night," a Sergeant says. (I thought that was the solution.)

We decide to get some eggs, just drive to the nearest farmhouse and demand them. The people tremble. They oblige at the double. I give a few cigarettes in return. A woman comes in and asks for quarters for the night. One of the millions of German refugees trying to make her way back home. She looks the hard type, smiles at me ostentatiously: I think of the joke ..... "Neither the time nor the b.......... inclination."

In MUNSTER I notice that the former German barracks are now an American camp. We drive in. "Can you fix us up with somewhere to sleep?" They take me into the officer's quarters. Then I have some coffee and doughnuts in the Red Cross.

Talk to some Yanks in camp. Everyone is full of how they are being teased by the German girls when they go swimming. "Allow us to rape them or shoot them," they demand, "we can't go on like this." I think of the times when I used to stand outside these self-same barracks enviously watching German soldiers drilling. Little I knew then that one day I should be sleeping in the officers' quarters together with the Yanks. There are Frenchmen, Poles, etc. in a nearby camp. They fraternize all right. I go to bed with the thought that morals have completely gone to blazes as far as German girls are concerned.

Second Day. Breakfast at 7 o' clock. Start off 07:45. Drive through MUNSTER. A heap of rubble. Not a soul in town except an occasional military policeman. Say goodbye to the Canadians, it was nice having them.

Towards PADERBORN. We find more and more people on the roads pushing handcarts, perambulators, carrying rucksacks, cycling. Everybody trying to get home: Poles, Russians, Dutchmen, Belgians, French, Jugoslavs and German evacuees. How they feed, house, etc. nobody can understand. The Germans usually wear little more than bathing costumes. Still, they are smart. Fill up with petrol in a Yankee Recce Unit. PADERBORN in complete ruins. Hardly a house intact.

Towards KASSEL. The scenery is beautiful. Generally, the villages are untouched, but occasionally one comes across one that is absolutely flat, then I comment, "There must have been a few snipers holding out here." The steel works in KASSEL are well hit. Town again in ruins. Amazing the amount of knocked-out German armored vehicles one sees around this district. The weather is still beautiful. The roads are usually very badly maintained.

Towards EISENACH. There we shall get on the Reichsautobahn. On the road we discover that one of our springs is broken, so pull up in EISENACH barracks, where there is an American Ordinance shop now. First, they don't feel like tackling the job. A bit of persuasion helps – wonderful tools they have and the way they set about the job. Inside an hour we have a complete new spring fitted and get greased up with a pneumatic grease-gun. Then on the Autobahn, wonderful driving now; just pull the hand accelerator and let the car go. Only, the temperature of the engine is getting too high, so we cut it out every time we go downhill. But the great sight of the Autobahn is "Europe going home." It's like an Exodus. There are just millions on the roads following this easy route. Occasionally, groups managed to have a truck. All groups fly their national colour, but, of course, the roads are dominated by the endless American transport that flows past.

EISENACH - GOTHA - JENA- WEIMAR At the famous cloverleaf cross, where the east-west

Autobahn meets the north-south, we get checked by American MPs. That was the only time we were checked on the whole journey. I still had my doubts as to whether some red tape wouldn't turn us back or arrest us. Everyone by now was highly surprised to see British troops.

Towards CHEMNITZ now, it is getting cooler. There are more Yankee patrols on the roads, but, of course, the Yanks and Russians only met in DRESDEN, according to information. We'll stay in CHEMNITZ and make inquiries there whether THERESIENSTADT is American or Russian, and what the chances are to get through the Russian lines.

Placard "Abfahrt Chemnitz," Yankee patrols who wave to us, and then masses of civilians lying on the roadside. Here is Chemnitz; white flags everywhere, 5 or 6 at every house. Why? Has the place only just been taken? There are no soldiers on the streets. Where is all the Yankee transport? Perhaps it's too late in the day. The Germans look at us in amazement. Wonder whether the place has been taken yet??! Suddenly, a lot of Russian soldiers. They don't look ex-prisoners to me. No, they have got weapons. The famous Russian Tommy gun! Gosh! we are in their lines already. Damn! A crowd of Cossacks in front of us. They wave wildly. That's better. Two officers ride up on horseback. They look grim. Silently they shake hands with us. I try my French. One understands. I look at him. He seems to be Jewish. "Seien Sie a Jid?" "A Jid, a Jid," he shouts. I ask him for the nearest American soldiers. He points in one direction, slaps me on the back, then we all salute and I ride away.

Two wires across the roads. This is the line, but the Russian and American sentry stand next to each other and try to chat. Without being asked, the Russian lowers the wires and we ride back into American territory. "What is the layout here?" I ask. "We get on fine," the Yank said. "They come to us to loot from the Germans because we don't do it so thoroughly, and we go to them because we can fraternize (i. e. sleep with German girls) over there. The line only exists for German soldiers and civilians."

I tell them that I want a letter in Russian explaining my business before crossing over for good. They send me up to Company HQ. There is the Batt. Colonel. I explain my business. He says, "You will have no difficulties at all. I'll give you the letter, but stay with me overnight; it's too late now to go on." I gladly accept his invitation. We set off to his HQ (CP in the American Army). I give a lift to a Yank ex-prisoner who has just got back. He says, "These Russians are the boys, they ought to rule the whole of Europe. The way they treat the Germans!!" Batt. CP is in a large modern villa. Ex-inhabitant was Herr Gotz, owner of several artificial silk factories and big estates. It is the most modern, comfortable and luxurious building I have ever seen. Everywhere glass, carpets and, if you want anything, just press a button.

In front of the HQ, a crowd of Germans collect who want help, information, favours, etc. The colonel chases them away. They make little move. He pulls his pistol; that works. They scatter. An American G. I. comes down the pathway with a Russian girl. We ask him, "Can you talk to her?" He grins, "No, but she knows what I want. She is terribly lively."

My driver and I have a bath. Marble bathrooms. It is too good to be true. The Yanks know how to run a place like this. It is spotless. When I come down again, a meal is waiting. Just now, Churchill starts his speech on the wireless. I listen whilst having my food. Gosh! I am hungry. That American Colonel is terrific; so are his officers. They are still working hard, though by now it is ten o' clock at night. Their problems are fantastic. I can hardly believe it. The Russians are letting all German prisoners, except SS and Officers, free and sending them home. If their homes are in Anglo-American hands, they cross over into our lines and get either turned back or arrested. Thousands of ex-allied prisoners are passing through every day and want to be catered to. German civilians are still fleeing from the Russians, who loot and rape to their heart's desire. The battalion is stretched out over 5 miles or more. How can one control it all? Our main topic is, "The Russians". These Yanks (all ranks) are dead against them. "What a queer crowd. Impossible to deal with. We arrange things with them one day, and the next day they absolutely take no notice of it at all." "Pig-headed just isn't the word. They have no system at all of how to treat the Germans. They never give the Germans a chance. I had a look at their weapons; they are good, but I still think we can beat them; if we don't do it now, we'll have to do it in ten years, and then they'll be producing their own transport. Remember what General Patton said, 'Let's bash on.' Easier to defend a line with bullets than this. Hope they pull us out and send a lot of diplomats here to sort things out. Give me the front line any day." I try to argue with them. We must not judge them by our standards.

12 o' clock. Tomorrow 3000 Jerry prisoners will have to be fed. Let's go down to the factory to inspect the kitchen. Herr Gotz is being rung up; he complains he is in bed. The Colonel asks him whether he wants to be fetched out with a riding whip. Then we go down. It is a huge factory. I interpret. Herr Gotz is dressed in a very well-cut suit. He leads us around. Then we start discussing things. He speaks English; subject switches to politics. Now he shouts at the top of

his voice and gesticulates, "I tell you, Stalin has won the war," he cries. "Here, under your very nose, the local Burgermeister published an order that nobody is to get food who doesn't belong to the Free German Party. He is a Communist. We go from one extreme into the other. Our people have lost everything; they'll become Communists." The Colonel says, "I am afraid so." Gotz cries, "How can Europe be healthy? Two wars in every generation." I remind him that it was usually Germany who started them.

"My children shall not stay in Europe, even if I lose millions." For everything, I have an answer, so he gets annoyed. "You are far too young, I can't talk with you." That gets me annoyed. I start fumbling with my pistol. He doesn't like it. We leave him and go back. The Yanks say, "He is right somehow." I don't agree. "Look at his and all Germans' conceit. Here am I, talking perfect German, and not once have they commented on it. They just think German is a Kultursprache and everybody ought to talk it perfectly. I am sick of them." We still have some wine and go to bed at one o' clock. What is going to happen to Europe if the Americans have so little understanding for the Russians? But I have never been so fond of the Yanks. The way they do things – that Colonel is a perfect chap.

<u>Third Day.</u> I wake up in the nursery of Herr Gotz' house. Hot bath again. Yankee breakfast.

Three eggs, but their food is too sweet for my liking. We are already again besieged by Jerries. "How can we get our property out of the Russian lines?" "Go back there! You started the war with Russia." "The Nazis did. What's happening about ........." In the end, we want to get some work done. We chase them away with riding whips. Europe, 1945 style. My jeep is being looked after. We load as much petrol as we can get on. The Colonel gives us a 10-in-1 ration that will last for a fortnight, I think. He says he'd love to come along himself. I wished he would. I decide to go back to ZWICKAU and make some more inquiries. Perhaps there are still German units fighting in the ERZ MOUNTAINS.

ZWICKAU: ruins again. Flat tire on the car, no time to stop. A Yankee workshop just gives us a new wheel. Grand blokes. Approach an American Captain on the street. "How is the road from here to PRAGUE?" "I don't think you'll have any difficulty! We have run a convoy into BRUX ourselves this morning. We have done it before. Have you got a flag?" "No, I haven't."

On the road to AUE, just past ZWICKAU, the American lines end. There is a barrier. We stop. There are German soldiers and civilians on the other side. We ask the guards, does he know where the Russians are? "Haven't seen any Russians yet; there are none in ERZGEBIRGE. IF you got to your destination and back, it will sure be as good as any Commando job you have done. Wish you good luck." Push on. Stop to inquire from German soldiers whether there are still units holding out in the mountains. Answer, "definitely no." A big civilian car overtakes us; there are two American officers in it. We follow them to AUE.

The town is still German. German police on the street. Thousands of German soldiers. I stand up in the jeep. They crowd around us; it is impossible to get through. "Are you coming or are the Russians? Can you take us prisoner?" After a while we manage to get moving again. The town is undamaged, unlooted. This is the last glimpse of Germany as it was. The Germans are well-dressed and well-fed. They look bitter and hard. Hysterical women are crying. A sinister people. Push on. I feel scared. Pick up a wounded German soldier and his girlfriend, who are going in our direction. That will afford some protection. I still fear mines. There are lots of roadblocks and perfectly good antitank guns covering them. But amongst all this, I am overawed by the beauty of the countryside around us. Steep mountains covered with tall and slim fir trees. The road winds through them. Occasional fast running rivulets. The German girl is small, round-faced, dark-haired and wears the traditional dress of the Erzgebirge: white blouse, gaily stitched with flowers, black frock, stitched again with all colours, square cloth braces. She looks terribly sweet and talks that very sweet local dialect. "This is a beautiful country," I say. "Ja, hier kommt's ei jeder zuruck der von hier weg geht." She gives us some sandwiches – natural honey! They leave us in SCHWARZENBERG. Beyond, the roads are lonely and deserted. People are cutting wood and tilling their scarce fields. My driver comments, "All this is no use to me; if ever we get back, nobody is going to believe me – all this."

Towards JOHANNGEORGENSTADT Now we are in Czech territory. Occasional Czech flags. People tell us that they are and feel German, these Sudeten, but they hope the Czech will save them from the Russians. Now we are on top of the ERZGEBIRGE, driving into a small village of 2,000 inhabitants. There are 15,000 German soldiers concentrated here. They still have their weapons. I pull up. Hundreds immediately collect around us. "What is this?" I enquire. "Sammelstelle Infantry Division." (Are you taking us prisoner?) There are thousands of German civilians with them, who try to evacuate Czechoslavkia before the revenge reaches them. They live in ditches and hedges. Again, I am besieged by crying women. "We cannot live under the Russians; they rob us." I answer, "Your soldiers have done the same in Poland, Russia, and Holland." Gosh! My heart stands still, what am I saying amongst 15,000 armed German soldiers? But they let it pass. "There are good and bad amongst every people." At last somebody comments on my excellent German. I tell them not to panic. Drive on slowly. Gosh! If I could loot here, I could make myself rich for the rest of my life just on gold and jewels, which every person, I am sure, is hiding somewhere. Everywhere, hard-faced German girls are lying around with their soldiers. Many wear trousers. There is a lot of charm and sex appeal about them. They look the sportive type. It's their eyes that are unnatural. Later, I was to learn that the German women just haven't got a mind of their own anymore. When they open their mouths, one might as well put on a record of Goebbels' propaganda. When they "make talk," they talk about "romantisch", "gute Musik," "Kultur," "ein bischen Seckt oder Schnaps." Now they look as if they just do not care anymore. On every army transport loaded with soldiers there are a few girls.

Drive on, join the main road: KARLSBAD - TREPLITZ SCHONAU near ST. JOACHIMTHAL. Two Yankees here tell us the Yanks are in KARLSBAD, also some Russians they met there. Three o' clock in the afternoon. The road is packed with German army transport, no sign of the Russians yet. Suddenly, British uniforms; ex-POWs trying to make their way back. Are they happy to see us!! We dish out fags. Tell them to make for KARLSBAD. Now we meet small groups every five minutes. Our fags go rapidly. Some look as if they had a rough time; others look very well. It depended on the camp they were in. Some have been on the road since Christmas. The Germans made them march 40 miles a day. They are full of horror tales, but all repeat, "But you want to see what they do to the Jews." "No punishment too hard for the Germans." Some are full of praise for the Russians. "Gave us their pistols so that we could get our own back on the Jerries." Other say, "Aren't the Russians queer? What a numb army!" Some have no good words for the Russians. We encourage them to make their way to KARLSBAD. They'll be flown home. They got enthusiastic. They tell us, "All the Czechs ask us to stay with them – prevents them from being looted by the Russians. Some of the boys are well settled in with families. Don't want to go home until they get proper transport." Many chaps were with girls. Don't blame them after prison. Some stole German transport, but Russians took it away from them again. The Russians are too short of transport themselves.

Again, along the roads, Europe is trekking home – every nationality, all ages, both sexes. KOMOTAU. Now we meet the Russian Army proper. "Stalin" and "T. 37" tanks. Lovely Russian field pieces. Long-barreled antitank guns and, apart from that, every conceivable type of cart, requisitioned all over Europe, a lot of it German.

The only regular Army transport is American or British-built. Everywhere, soldiers with the famous Russian Tommy gun. I am standing in the car all the time now. Wave to every group I see. They wave and cheer back. The Military Police (mostly girls) even salute smartly. They carry two flags, and wave the traffic onwards with them. There is no traffic discipline, consequently one gets the most awful traffic jams. Then every officer gets out and there is a lot of shouting, gesticulating and generally a lot of energy is spent. It all seems futile, but suddenly the whole thing moves on again. Uphill – downhill, we have no brakes, escape a collision by inches. It is just one prolonged nightmare. Now there are Russians everywhere and thousands of Germans prisoners. BRUX, DUX. Some excellent bombing was done here. Czechoslovakia looks hollow. Huge shops empty – it's worse than Holland. Civilians stop us on the road – "Why haven't you come here? Rather have you." Damn them, they are Germans anyhow, I think. TREPLITZ SCHONAU. People tell me that the Ghetto in THERESIENSTADT is still intact. No last minute mass executions.

The Russians drive on a very low grade diesel fuel. Their exhausts emit black clouds of smoke. Horrible driving. Some lorries are broken down. The drivers get out and work with terrific energy with their simple hand tools. There is no stopping until the job is done. Convoys of "Panjecarts" move along. They move and move without interruption, until they get to their destination. The horses occasionally drop dead, then new horses are fetched from the nearest farmer. One sees many dead horses, but the small Russian horses stand up well to this treatment. When the men rest, the horses are just let loose, the soldiers look as if there is nothing they didn't know about horses. The way they hold the reins says everything.

Road diversion. We are now on the main road, TREPLITZ SCHONAU - PRAG. A Russian woman MP asks in English, "Are you American?" "No, English." It occurs to me that she might speak German better. She is thrilled and says in German, "British Officer speaks German; like me spreche alle Sprachen." Then she embraces me. Nearly strangles me. The Russian girls are not particularly good to look at, but there is something about them that makes them attractive. One cannot see it in pictures, but I realize it now that I see the live being in front of me.

At last, THERESIENSTADT. Civilians show the way to the Ghetto. I always thought I would die with excitement at this moment, but I am pretty cool now, only that queer feeling in the pit of the stomach which I get before a parachute jump. Check guards outside the camp (just a part of the town); I tell them what I want. First, they jump to attention, then a Captain comes. He says, "If your parents are in the part where there is typhus, promise me that you'll come back." "I promise."

Slowly, we drive through the barrier. I stand on the front seat of the jeep leaning over the screen. I realize what a moment this is. It might have been a scene in Lordship Garden, London, on Saturday afternoon. There are people – Jews – in the thousands everywhere. They look undernourished, overworked, but fairly well dressed. Western Europe's Jews- every face seems to be familiar. They are all ages, but every eye reflects senility and tiredness. What a grim sight!! I cannot even force myself to smile at them. Everybody crowds around. Drive on carefully. Some are too weak to get out of the way quickly. This is the way we drove into the liberated towns of France, Belgium and Holland.

The crowds were the same, but what a different atmosphere! I think of Wordsworth's lines: -

> Alas, there is no hope, no tears
> Nor that content surpartial wealth
> That sage in meditation found.

All eyes are on us, but they are too stunned to utter a sound. I can only look at them grimly. Stop in front of the Registration office. There is one girl still working. I demand my parents' address. She answers in English, probably learned throughout the empty days of the concentration camps. The Jewish spirit is indomitable. She gets terribly excited. "They are really still here. Are you lucky!! I must go with you myself, though I nearly die with excitement." Outside, my driver is besieged. We can hardly get through the crowds now. Where do all these people live? What a terrible overcrowding! Light inside some of the windows reveal beds and tables made out of raw wood. Everywhere there are double, triple bunks. Stop! This is the house. The girl inquires. My parents are having supper on the balcony. I send her forward and wait in the corridor. Human beings everywhere! No privacy here! I am getting slightly excited. Damn it, I have jumped out of aeroplanes. I am not going to let this get me down! That does the trick. Still looking grim with my arms crossed over my chest.

The next minutes are indescribable. I suddenly find myself in their arms. They are both crying wildly. It nearly sounds like the crying of despair. I look at Father, and in spite of having prepared myself for a lot, I have to bite my teeth together not to show my shock. He is hardly recognizable! Completely starved and wrecked. My first regular thoughts after a few minutes are, "What a grim show." The next, our old Commando watch word,

"Don't panic!" I lead them to the balcony and force them to sit down. They still can't utter a word for crying. Some of their friends, fine people, come to calm them down. Now at last I manage a smile. People rapidly collect in the yard beneath the balcony. They shout, "Congratulations" and "Mazeltow" to my parents. Now they are cheering. That settles my parents. Father is completely calmed down now – one look into his eyes convinces me that his spirit is completely unbroken. He is still the old realistic idealist he always has been. During the next few hours I have all reasons to admire him. Mother looks aged, but tanned and fit. There is still a lot of youth about her. (Damn it, I haven't learned to go about with girls for nothing.) All the most prominent people – who mean so much to my parents – come to congratulate them. The news must be spreading like wildfire. A lot of young girls come to bring us bouquets. Mother, as a good housewife, puts them all into water. I've just got to get back to normal thinking. I remember we haven't eaten or drunk anything since 7 o' clock that morning. It is now 8 o' clock at night. I fetch the driver up. Mother is all for him, he is a nice London kid, and full of understanding. We have lots of ersatz coffee. Somebody produces matzoth, saved from Pesach! Mother has Kartoffel Knodle. Talking about their past, our relatives, the world at large, we all feel very happy now.

Later, I go to see the Russian Commandant. He is just holding a meeting with his staff and some camp leaders. I give him my explanatory letter. He asks me whether or not I have found my parents. Then he tells me that he is going to close the whole camp the next day as a precautionary measure. He tells me not to sleep in the camp, also that he has to close both eyes for even letting me out again. He asks me whether I am inoculated. He and his three women doctors give the impression of great efficiency. He is very firm on the point of leaving as soon as possible – can't be helped.

The driver decides to sleep in the open in the jeep. The Russian guards wouldn't let him out of the camp anymore. He is being besieged by people who want news from relatives in England. They have obviously cracked up. We promise to take letters back. Now at last we get some quiet – I have no intention to sleep at all.

A small circle gathers on the balcony. Somebody produces red wine. It is dark now. There are stars in the sky and it is warm. Many people sleep in the open. We talk and talk. They tell me of the horrors they have gone through. Is there any need to repeat them here, after all the accounts in the press? Still it strikes me much harder now. My parents have been in BELSEN. Out of 137,000 who have gone through the camp here, there are still 23,000 alive. One day, practically all girls under 14 were gassed. In the last moment, the SS tried to gas everybody, but some SS Commandant managed to postpone the whole thing for 24 hours. Next day, the Russians came in. Everybody tries to avoid the ghastly tales. Good psychologists and Jewish spirit have seen to it that these people have not acquired prison minds.

Mainly they want to know about the outside world. My parents live in the Dutch colony, and Holland is the main topic. I tell them about the enormous British war efforts, D-Day, the heavy fighting in France, Walcheren, the endless winter in Holland, starvation, the complete ruin that was Germany, the Yankee army, etc. Somebody writes everything down for publication in the camp. They have been completely cut off for ages. Everybody wants to know about Palestine, they didn't know about the Jewish Brigade.

They empty a room for us. We continue sitting there with electric light. Father nearly cries when I give him several hundred English cigarettes. That will make him a millionaire here, he says. At 2 o' clock people at last leave us alone. We open that huge box of American 10-to-1 rations. Even to me they look a treasure. My parents just can't believe their eyes. They nearly have a bad conscience about accepting them. At 3 o' clock they, too, go to bed. I doze. What a misery! I could cry all night. As Father said, "We can never pay them back." What hope is there? I try to reason it out. The young ones will pull through, no doubt. Most of them, except Germans, want to go back to their respective countries. The rest hope for Palestine. Will they be let in by the English? Will a nationalistic policy that cares for the maintenance of the healthy only not spoil the last hopes of these poor individuals? My parents, too, want to go to Palestine, but to Holland for recuperating first. For many, there is that tremendous question whether the liberated countries will let stateless Jews back into their territory. And above all, there hovers for me only (not for them) that great question, "Will it be peace with Russia?"

FOURHT DAY. I can't sleep. I get up at 6 o' clock and shave. Mother comes in at the same time. The driver is up too. Many people in camp seem to have lost sleep altogether. We have breakfast outside again. American rations this time, but I can't eat. Mail comes pouring in now. A woman sorts it out for me. For an hour or so I discuss with the leader of the Dutch Jews what can be done. We discuss plans, ways of communicating. He is Professor Meyer from the Hague Peace Palace. He, too, looks a wreck, but his mind is completely unaffected. His daughter and three others left the camp two days ago before quarantine to walk back to Holland. Some people beg us to take them out. This is out of the question. I even have my doubts whether the

Russians will let us out. At the last moment a man approaches me, and says, "I own three engineering factories. If you make your way here, you can do anything. I offer you directorship of all three factories." I point out that I will still have to stay in the army for two years. He is unperturbed, gives me his address and tells me to think it over.

Things are getting exciting again. At 10 o' clock I tell the driver secretly to pull up in front of the house. Letters are still pouring in. Some people beg frantically to get favours. In a small room I say goodbye to my parents, away from the crowds, then I rush downstairs, jump on the jeep and drive to the gate at top speed. The guard looks doubtful. I say, "Engle Offizier," so he shakes hands and opens the gate.

Standing in the jeep, we chase once along the outside of the camp to show my parents that we got out all right. Then we are off.

Towards KARLSBAD, hundreds of ex-POWs on the road, American and British. I carefully only pick up those who look as if they have had a rough time. One American, just a bundle of bones in rags of a uniform, is nearly broken down. Poor boy. In a few hours from now he will be in comfort. We have nothing to help them. All fags, food and spare clothing we left behind in the camp. Still no brakes on the jeep, but roads are emptier now. Every time we want to halt, we all jump out and pull the jeep back.

3 o' clock. We have made it back to KARLSBAD and American lines. We are told to deposit our POW's in ELBOGEN. Drive there. Just manage to get there in time to get them on some lorries going to NURNBERG aerodrome. Tomorrow morning they'll be home in England. Good luck to them.

I amble about in a hotel. American Battalion Officers Mess. Here I will stay till tomorrow and have a rest. The Americans were tired; they are overworked. The whole of Europe seems to be going home through their lines. Impossible to handle the crowds.

At about 5 p. m., a German general comes in with a Czech patriot and a German soldier. He wants to surrender his 15,000 men, who are still in ERZGEBIRGE. The American Colonel tells him to go to the Russians. I interpret. In the end, the Colonel decides to take the General to the Russian Divisional Commander (I am afraid I forgot the name of that Russian General, and I never enquired for the number of the division). We drive down to KARLSBAD. Div. HQ is in a huge hotel. The Russians have been notified of our arrival. The American Colonel speaks a passable Russian. He is a huge, fine-looking, hefty chap of about 30 years. He is one of the few Americans who has been in the Commando Battle School in Scotland, and he proudly told me that he managed to outlast it. He wears lots of campaign medals - N. Africa, Sicily, Normandy,

France, Germany- and lots of bravery medals. We get on fine together.

A Russian Colonel and Major receive us. They, like most Russians soldiers, have lots of medals. The Colonel (Chief of Staff of the division) wears the Order of Lenin. The whole thing is terribly informal. There is a Russian-German interpreter, a Jewish staff sergeant (I am beginning to learn Russian ranks). He never loses his sense of humor. We are cracking jokes all the time. The Russian G. I. is particularly happy. I notice that the guard does not stand to attention as we enter. The Russians, in their happiness, make no distinction between us and the Germans. First, we are led in to have a huge dinner. The food that follows is too fantastic for words. People will get envious if I describe it. More Russian officers participate. They are as happy as children. Champaign flows in buckets. The Germans (in the meantime, an ugly piece of a German colonel arrives) protest, they haven't eaten for 3 days; they will not be able to stand the alcohol: the Russians take no notice. The war is over now; we all ought to be brothers. Russian girls serve. They have no idea how to do that neatly. I am too hungry for caring too. The champagne swells my head. That must have been my third bottle. Still, we toast Anglo-American Russian friendship. Churchill – Stalin – Roosevelt. The Germans just have to join in. The situation is just too funny for words. That German general looks stupid. He is probably very thorough. In his heart he is a weakling, I am sure; therefore, he is a show of militarism, but by gum, next to these brilliant vivid Russians with their sparkling good-natured eyes, he fades like a candle before a searchlight. I tell the American colonel, "No wonder they lost the war with such generals." He agrees. When I put him opposite Mills Roberts (1 Commando Brigade), I have to laugh. He lacks the individuality of the British, the efficiency of the Americans and the brilliance of the Russians. Against that, he has German thoroughness.

Sudeten German waiters serve the drinks. They look sour. The Russian colonel tells them to be more enthusiastic about serving the Great Soviet Army. An awkward scene arises: I thought we were going to witness a shooting, but the waters calmed down again.

We are led up to the general. Two huge doors open. The American colonel and I enter first. The whole party follows after us. We all stand in line and salute. The general salutes back, then he comes forward and shakes hands with the American and me only; he asks us to sit down. He is a simple- looking, round-faced man, but has thin lips, and he beams discipline and energy. He is a "Hero of the Soviet Union." Now follows the most to – the – point conference I have ever attended. The Russian knows exactly what he wants from the Germans. He is obviously used to handling any big problem. He has the clearest and most mathematical mind ever. The German is no match for him. We are mere spectators. He tells the Germans where they have to march for food. The Germans complain it is too far to be done in a day. The Russian retorts that they should get used to the standards of the Russian Army. We all get up and salute again. He shakes hands with the American and me and thanks us for our help. We leave. That is the last I saw of the Russian Army. My final judgment is: the Russians have very fine fighting equipment. Where we put our organization and administration, they put the tremendous effort and enthusiasm of the individual. Outwardly, they seem to have little discipline, but let nobody make any mistake, <u>they are soldiers to the bone,</u> not a rabble of badly organized recruits. Their fantastic, pig-headed efforts may become the stumbling block of the world, but it was their salvation.

Sleep in one hotel room together with a good-looking Dutch woman and two Dutchmen. Europe 1945. But everybody seemed to keep to their respective beds.

<u>FIFTH DAY.</u> Push off early. EGER. Brakes are repaired. Busy town. The Americans are broadcasting orders with loud speakers.

Hof-Autobahn towards JENA. Go into a German farmhouse and demand to participate in their meal. One girl sits alone. She is Russian, speaks good German. I talk to her for about an hour. She is not good looking, but that is that Russian something? She comes from the Black Sea. Waiting and longing to get back to her communal farm. "These Germans are terrible," she states, disinterested. "Never happy, always nagging and grumbling. They are a hopeless lot; anyhow there are so many better people in the world, hardly worthwhile to take any notice of them. It is as if I had known you for years. Come and see me on our communal farm at the Black Sea." Off again to MUNSTER that night. All the Yankees are interested in our adventures. I hardly get any sleep for telling tales.

SIXTH DAY. Call on the A. M. G. in BORKEN. See one captain, who sits in our former drawing room. I tell him who I am. He is a nice chap and most surprised; asks me to apply to be transferred into his staff. We discuss his work at length. I have a look at the Germans working for him. I don't like them. Don't know them either. He takes me to the nearest AMG HQ. I promise to apply.

`Back to GOES. Tomorrow I shall see the Netherlands Government.

May 45.

US Holocaust Memorial Museum

**Arrival of Dutch Jews in Terezin. This is from the Nazi
film "Der Fuehrer schenkt den Juden eine Stadt". (The
Fuehrer gives the Jews a town as a present)
To produce this film about 24 thousand prisoners
were transferred from Terezin to the Death Camps
to hide the overcrowding. The film was shot by a
Czech Marketing Company on orders from the SS.
But the film crew shot a lot of pictures which they
never gave to the SS.**

US Holocaust Memorial Museum

**Arrival of Dutch Jews in Terezin. Note the cart of loaves on the picture to give the impression that there was ample food for the camp.**

US Holocaust Memorial Museum

**Food rations being distributed.**

US Holocaust Memorial Museum

## Arrival of Dutch Jews in Terezin

# Liberation and Army of Occupation

When I returned from my six-day trip to Terezin, my unit, 41 Royal Marine Commando, was still in the southern part of Holland. I wrote the Terezin story in just one night. One of the office sergeant orderlies of the Commando, who like myself, had been with the unit since D-Day, then typed the whole report and made 14 copies on one of those ink duplicating machines which we had in those days. He said: ""This is an historic document," and he kept one copy for himself. I did not think of it that way; I just wanted copies to send to relatives and friends.

The temporary seat of the Dutch Government was in Breda, not too far from my unit. I went there and found the Department for Repatriation. I had a letter addressed to Princess Juliana from a judge of the Peace Court in the Hague, who was the head of the Dutch "colony" in Terezin. A lovely young lady in the Repatriation Department offered to take me to Princess Juliana. The weather was beautiful as we drove into the Royal Estate not too far from Breda in our open jeep. I met Juliana, gave her the letter and, she told me to make an appointment with her adjutant. I could not keep that appointment, because by that time we had moved into Germany, of all places, my hometown Borken!

Nobody believes that I had nothing to do with the destination of this move. Our occupation duties were very light: the purpose was to outfit us with new weapons for the invasion of Japan. 41 Commando had been in the invasion of Sicily, Normandy and Walcheren; no way was there going to be an invasion of Japan without us.

Being back "home" as the undisputed victor in a town whose inner city had been totally destroyed, and from where I had left as a despised "untermensch," could have been a very emotional experience, if I had had any emotions in those days. We confiscated and lived in the most beautiful patrician houses, homes to which Jews would never have been invited, even in pre-Hitler times. We had our new weapon demonstrations and drills on the soccer field, from which Jews were previously banned, even as spectators, in the mid-30's. We practiced our new attack tactics in the woods near the town, which had been totally unsafe for Jews, even for peaceful walks, in the Nazi era. We ordered the town administration to restore the open-air swimming pool, which had been strictly "off limits" to Jews.

Some people recognized me, but if I did not want to talk to them, I told them to get off British-confiscated property. Some people I approached myself, including my favorite teacher, Herr Tinnefeld, who had really done his level best to shield us, the Jewish students, in the public High School. My father's ex-secretary came to see me after I chanced across her brother. The town sent me a delegation to exert my influence for the release of the county executive (Landrat), who, they claimed, at great personal risk had prevented the killing of Jews in the Kristallnacht in November 1938.

I recognized the original SS man and I had him arrested. I ran into Dr. Damen, the biology teacher, who became an enthusiastic Nazi as soon as Hitler took power and who taught "Rassenkunde,"-the science of races, a blatant vehicle for teaching anti-Semitism. In the thirties, my cousin, Charley Gans, my brother Gershon and I "gave him hell" when he taught that garbage in our classes. Now Dr. Damen approached me to facilitate his reinstatement; he pointed out that if he had reported the arguments we gave him to the Gestapo, our fathers would have landed in jail. I sent word back to him, saying, "I don't hold you responsible for the millions of Allied soldiers and civilians who were killed in the war. I do not even hold you responsible for the killing of six million Jews. But the two hundred German soldiers from this town who lost their lives as a result of Hitler's insane wars, my ex-classmates, they are on your conscience."

There were a lot of other incidents, some amusing, some quite grim. The seat of the County Military Government was in our house, which had been Gestapo headquarters during the war, taken over after my parents left in 1939 (The house is there to this day). The British Military Commandant asked me to join his staff, but I had no desire to do that.

One day my cousin, Herbert Jonas, came to Borken to see his old home. Someone told him that I was in town and in which house we, the Commando officers, lived. Herbert was a US paratrooper. He had been at the American front in Belgium, Christmas, 1944, when Hitler launched his desperate last counter attack (the Battle of the Bulge). Like thousands of other US troops, Herbert's unit was cut off, but when his unit decided to surrender, he refused to go along and stealthily infiltrated back into the US lines through the German lines with two other US soldiers.

For the crossing of the river Rhine, Herbert landed by parachute near Wesel and was injured before Muenster, all places with which we were so familiar in our youth. Now he was back with his unit, stationed in the Ruhr District, and so we met again in our hometown, after having parted in 1938.

Two weeks after we had moved to Borken, a driver and I drove from Borken to The Hague.

Roads in Holland were hardly damaged and there was no traffic. We drove from Borken to The Hague in three hours, where I found my lovely young lady (whom I had dated a few times in between), who had moved to the Hague with the rest of the Dutch government. She told me that she had taken care of everything: the Dutch "colony" from Terezin was to be flown back home by airplane the following week. That's how my parents came to Eindhoven. There they came across one of the Loewenstein girls from Ahaus near Borken, who had been hiding in Holland during the war and was now working with the British. She persuaded a British officer to send me a letter through army channels, whereupon I went to Eindhoven the following Erev Shabbat (Friday) to meet my parents, loaded with some good German chickens, which "happened to come across my way." The parents were living in the house (with the family) where the Loewenstein girl had been hidden. They were out when I arrived, but when, on their return, they saw the jeep before the house, my mother said immediately: "He is here!"

**The market place in Borken. June 1945, the town
was completely destroyed, in one night, before the
assault of the British troops.
The house with the stepped façade, was the pre
war Rathaus, (Municipal building)**

**Another street in Borken in June 1945. The house on the left used to be the kosher butcher in town.**

**In front of our house which had been Gestapo headquarters during the war, and now was the headquarter of the county Military Government. June 1945.**

**In front of our house. June 1945.**

**With Andrew Kershaw in Reklinghausen**

**Fall of 1945. Parents and Grandmother Fraenkel in front of their house in Zandvoort, Holland on the occasion of Theo's first visit.**

## Professor Bram Gans

Back to the day when I visited my lady friend in the Repatriation Department of the Dutch government in the Hague. After lunch with my lady friend, we drove off to Leyden. Jack Gans, whose beautiful home in York in England had been the rallying point of all the Gans and Deleuwe soldiers in the Dutch, British and American armies, had urged me to find his brother, Professor Bram Gans in Leyden. Bram was a Professor of Psychiatry, and was a personal friend of Albert Einstein.

I drove to the police headquarters in Leyden and said, "Take me to the hiding place of Professor Gans. I am sure you know where it is." After some discussion in Dutch, which they thought I could not understand, they detailed one policeman to ride with me. He took me to a house on the outskirts of Leyden. I told my driver to take the policeman back to his office. A very nice lady received me in the house. She told me that Professor Gans had gone for a walk, but that I should wait in his room upstairs. The room was lined with books on bookshelves on all four walls from the floor to the ceiling. A door led to a small balcony. After looking at some of the books, I noticed, by chance, a leg on the floor of the balcony. I went outside and saw a man who looked so much like Jack Gans, that I had no doubt that he was Bram Gans.

I thought he had fainted so I bent over him, to see whether he was breathing. He opened his eyes, saw the pistol on my belt and said in German, "Have you come to arrest me?" I laughed (shows how little feelings we had in those days) and said in English, "No, I am a British officer, not a German officer, and I am Manfred Gans, the son of your cousin Moritz. Your brother Jack and his wife Annie asked me to find you,"

We went inside and he told me about his years in hiding and some of the atrocities the Germans had perpetrated in Leyden, including the killing of one of his Indonesian assistants, whom they regarded as a "Nigger." When my jeep returned, we drove to the house of his daughter, who had also emerged from hiding.

That afternoon on our way back to Germany I stopped over at some other distant relatives whose address I had.

## Grandmother Bertha Fraenkel

A few days later, on a Sunday, I drove from Borken to the northern Dutch town, Leewarden. This time, I took along two of my Marine Commando friends, who wanted a change from the rubble and destruction of Germany.

My parents had given me the address of the place where my grandmother was living in hiding, while I was in Terezin, and my aunts in Israel and Kenya had urged me to find their mother. My grandmother was very popular with all her grandchildren. We all had spent many vacations in her house in Voelksen near Hanover, with or without our parents. "Oma" loved to play cards with us for money, and she made us work in her garden, where she grew the world's best strawberries. She also had a terrific sense of humor.

Again, the weather was brilliant and the roads were totally empty. There was just one bridge, of dubious stability, which we had to cross near Groeningen; in their retreat, the Germans had attempted to do as much harm as possible. On the way out of Leewarden to the village where Oma lived on a farm, I stopped to ask some people whether we were going in the right direction, and a woman said, "I am sure you have come for Oma."

And so we met again.... As we drove into this relatively poor, but very neat farm, the excitement of the farmer and his family showed through, in spite of all the Dutch reserve. This is what they had been waiting for: Oma knew that I was in the British Army from the Red Cross letter I had sent to my parents in 1941, before they all had to go into hiding, but she did not even have the addresses of her daughters.

After the initial excitement, Oma resumed her knitting and I brought her up to date on what everybody in the family was doing. They served us some malt-based coffee. This farm tried to be completely self sufficient; they even made their own cigars from a leafy plant they grew, and they spun their own wool. Later that summer, I spent a few days there with my parents. We returned to our unit the same evening.

### Occupation and the End of the War

In July, we moved from Borken to Reklinghausen, on the northern edge of the Ruhr District, where our main task was to guard a prisoner camp for high-ranking Nazis, Gestapo members, unsavory concentration camp guards and similar "automatic arrest" categories.

We also had to patrol one section of the town by night to enforce the curfew. I persuaded everyone to patrol silently in rope shoes or sneakers; that way we caught more violators. Actually, the Germans were very grateful for these patrols, because gangs of ex-slave workers, roaming by night, would occasionally attack homes for loot and rape.

We used a carefully selected gang of our prisoners to reactivate the tennis courts in the municipal park of the town, and that was where I learned to play tennis.

Again we lived in comfortable homes, started to employ German cooks, which improved the quality of our food tremendously, and we had an officers' club in the beer cellar of the Rathaus, complete with a very flexible German band, who could harmonize with all our bawdy songs.

One night, Andrew Kershaw (my best friend from 3 Troop, who had joined 41 Commando when we returned from the Walcheren invasion) woke me up and said, "The Americans have dropped an atom bomb on a town in Japan. One bomb wiped out a whole town." I said, "I don't believe them," turned around and went back to sleep. Next morning at breakfast, we all listened to the BBC news intensely, and we agreed that that this was the end of the war.

The following Sunday, Andrew and I drove to Eindhoven, where my parents still lived. My father's oldest sister and her husband were there for a visit. My aunt and uncle had survived the war in hiding, but two of their sons, one daughter-in-law and one of their grandchildren had perished in Concentration Camps.

In spite of all the cruelties, hardships and deprivations they had experienced and all that might have been in store for Andrew and me, my mother did not like the idea of the atom bomb at all. "Some one is going to misuse it."

Shortly thereafter, my parents returned to the town where they had lived before going into hiding, Zandvoort. The chief of police, with whom they had been friends, arranged for them to rent a very nice home at 11 Regentesseweg.

The British Army now started to prepare for demobilization. A policy was evolved whereby no one was to stay in the services for more than six years, so we could all calculate our dates of demobilization (for us the war had started in 1939, and conscription started a few months before the war).

I was put in charge of a program for preparing soldiers for civilian life. We were told to organize classes in mathematics and writing and vocational courses in carpentry, bricklaying, welding etc. I was sent to a course for teaching mathematics near Emden in North Germany and there, in my spare time, I learned sailing small race boats. Then I was sent for another few days to a mathematics teaching course in Brusselles and had a chance to enjoy opera performances and the nightlife.

## Gershon

My brother Gershon, who had been with the British Army in Italy, came to visit me in Reklinghausen. We had not seen each other for ten years. He had the complexion of desert exposure; he also had successfully taken a small boatload of Jewish displaced persons from Italy to British Palestine for illegal immigration. I took him on a short trip to our hometown, Borken, and arranged for our 2nd in command, Major Cunningham, to bring him to our parents in Zandvoort. There was no way of warning the parents of such visits, so the excitement was great. Major Cunningham arranged for Gershon to go over to England to visit our brother Teo, who was working on a farm in Yorkshire. Teo was so stunned by this unexpected visit that after just saying "hello," he turned back to his work to slowly digest what was happening.

On Gershon's return to Holland, I met him in Zandvoort. A few days later, I took him to the South of Germany, from where he returned to his unit in Italy. I had given him my German submachine gun for the fight which was undoubtedly coming (We, who had done the actual fighting, were always loaded with German weapons, which could be sold for a lot of money to those who had never been close to an armed enemy). Gershon returned to Israel and was "demobilized" soon thereafter.

## Persecution, Acquisitions and Betrayal

At the end of the war, all the Jews who returned from concentration camps, from hiding or from exile were faced with the major task of recuperating their assets, businesses, houses, apartments and belongings. Under the stress of war, people in almost all European countries had bought at bargain prices, or had helped themselves freely to those possessions of the Jews that had not been confiscated by local Nazi organizations or by the German authorities. The fight for the recuperation of Jewish assets went on for years, even for those Jews who, like my parents, actually returned to their former hometowns.

My parents had lived in the Dutch ocean resort Zandvoort since 1939. They had made a lot of friends, including the Chief of the Zandvoort police, Mr. Vreeman, who immediately after the war helped them to find a house for rent. There was a housing shortage in Zandvoort, because the Germans had destroyed several rows of houses along the seafront to give their guns a free range of fire in case of an Allied landing.

When the systematic arrest of Jews and their deportation to concentration camps had started in 1941, my parents had gone into hiding in the north of Holland on a farm near Leeuwarden. They had brought from Germany some beautiful, custom-made living room and dining room furniture, which they now had to "park" with non-Jewish friends. Similarly, they had to dispose of beds and bedroom furniture.

Valuables such as gold watches, diamond rings, jewelry, gold coins, certificates of international shares and bonds posed a major problem for safe hiding, but my father had become friendly with a detective, Mr. Smouters, who had been introduced to him by my cousin Alfred de Leeuw. Smouters and Alfred had become friends during their compulsory military service in the Dutch army. Smouters had now become part of the insipient "underground" resistance against the German occupation. My parents decided to "park" all their valuables in a special strong box with Mr. Smouters.

After his return to Zandvoort, my father contacted Smouters and asked him to return the strong box. Smouters, who by now had been promoted to the rank of Political Detective, sent word back that he had given the strong box to Alfred, because Alfred was in a pretty safe hiding place. But Alfred and his family were caught, and Alfred died of starvation in a concentration camp, having given all his food to his wife and daughter, who both survived.

I was due for a few days leave (furlough) in the summer of 1945, and instead of going back to England, I had a jeep take me to Zandvoort. Two days later, my parents and I went by train up the West coast of the Zuider Zee. Train services in Holland had only just been restored, and the trains that ran were terribly overcrowded. At the end of this narrow coast line the train stopped at a ferryboat terminal near Den Helder, where we changed to a roomy ferryboat that took us across the Zuider Zee. (By now, 2006, there is no more Zuider Zee; it has been pumped empty and converted into farmland and towns. A new network of roads and railways has been created).

The ferryboat docked on the eastern shores of the Zuider Zee, from where we could have taken another train to bring us to Leeuwarden and other towns of northern Holland. However, as arranged, Mr. Smouters was waiting for us with his car. Since he was a "big shot," he was one of the very few officials who could run a car in gasoline-starved Europe. He took us to the farm where my grandmother had been in hiding and where she still lived and where I had visited her a few weeks earlier. This was the first time my parents and my grandmother met since my parents had been arrested and shipped off to concentration camp. But during the years of hiding, my parents had become very good friends with this small but very independent farmer and his large family. So this was a happy and exciting reunion.

Smouters proposed that he would come back the following day to take us to his girlfriend, Dr. Dykstra. My parents were aware of this relationship already before they went into hiding; they had met Dr. Dykstra and they knew that

Smouters was not living any more with his wife and children. It had been my father's plan to confront Smouters in the presence of Dr. Dykstra.

My mother had no intention of going with us for that confrontation. She only warned "not to disappear into one of the many canals."

Smouters came the following afternoon and drove us to Dr. Dykstra, a very impressive, tall, blond woman, who was in charge of a sanatorium comprising a hospital, a psychiatric ward and an old age home. After being shown around, we went to Dr. Dykstra's apartment for afternoon tea. Soon my father indicated that he wanted to discuss the fate of the strong box that he had given to Smouters before going into hiding. Smouters maintained that he had given the box to my cousin Alfred, whose hiding place was regarded as very secure. My father then revealed that he had met Alfred in the Bergen-Belsen concentration camp, that Alfred had never mentioned anything about a box and Alfred was too conscientious a person to withhold such important information from his uncle. Smouters stuck to his tale.

Eventually, my father told Smouters that he realized that during the war everybody was short of money and that he could well understand that Smouters had "hocked" such items as the gold watch, jewelry and pieces of gold, but there was nothing anybody could do with the stocks and bonds. There was no stock exchange trading during the war, and the Dutch government had declared any transfer of such papers made during the war as illegal. He was willing to forget about all the valuables, as long as all the papers were returned.

Smouters said that we were making a very serious accusation, but he would do anything in his power to find all the lost items. He then recorded an exact description of all the items in his notebook. Dr. Dykstra claimed that Smouters could not have taken anything since he was always broke.

In the late afternoon, Smouters brought us back to the farm and that was the last we ever saw of him.

Soon thereafter, my father happened to meet Mr. Vreeman, the Chief of Police of Zandvoort, who remarked, "You were always such good friends of Smouters; do you still see him?" My father then told the whole story of the strong box to Vreeman, who was most interested. He said that during the war the local underground had accumulated weapons in a well-hidden cache. When in May, 1945, the call came to rise against the Germans and their local Nazi allies, they had opened the cache and found it empty. They soon found out that someone had sold their weapons to the Communist underground. They suspected Smouters.

Vreeman then offered to use one of his local detectives to find all those items that might have been sold to a local pawnshop. The detective sat down with my mother and father to get an exact description of all the valuables. Within a few days, he found some of the jewelry and had proof that it had been pawned by Smouters.

My father then engaged a high-powered lawyer to sue Smouters, and in the winter of 1945/46, on one of my visits to Zandvoort, we went to see this lawyer in Amsterdam.

Within a very short time, the lawyer informed my father that the case was hopeless: Smouters with all his political connections could not be "touched." There were only two Political Detectives in Holland, and Smouters was one of them. Their task was to find hidden Nazi collaborators.

The case now seemed hopeless, but a few months later, Holland had its first post-war national election and our lawyer became the Minister of the Interior. Two days later, Smouters was arrested. Naturally, the government's case against him dealt with more profound matters than my parents' valuables. Dr. Dykstra testified to his good character to no avail; he was sentenced to ten years restricted service in

Indonesia, which at that time was still a Dutch colony.

My parents always suspected that Smouters, surreptitiously, had informed the Nazis authorities of their hiding place; conceivably, he also betrayed the very secure hiding place of Alfred.

## More than Assets

I started the above Chapter with the sentence, "At the end of the war, all the Jews who returned from concentration camps, from hiding or from exile were faced with the major task of recuperating their assets, businesses, houses, apartments and belongings." Alas, some of these returnees had to find their children first and our family was no exception to these events of tragedy and redemption.

My father had four brothers and five sisters. His youngest brother was our favorite: Uncle Ernst. who was not yet married during most of our youth, and with his positive, self-confident, out-going attitude, showered his nephews and nieces with gifts at all possible opportunities.

Uncle Ernst married Suse Klein in 1935 and their first child, Ruth, was born in 1936. They lived in Hamburg, where Ernst was in business with his brother Sally (father of now Prof. Carl Gans and Leo Gans) Both Sally and Ernst left with their families, after Kristallnacht, November 9th, 1938.

Sally settled in New York and Ernst went to Amsterdam, where his son Karel, was born in 1939.

After the German invasion of Holland in May 1940, life for Jews became steadily worse; Jews were not allowed to own businesses, they were not allowed into parks and other recreational facilities, they had to wear the Yellow Star, and at night the Germans would randomly round up Jews to take them to an old theater, which became known as The Joodse (Jewish) Schouwburg. from where they were sent to concentration camps.

In the words of then 5-year-old Ruth Gans:

*"Our life was extremely restricted. I was very conscious of having to wear a yellow star"*

To avoid being rounded up, Ernst, Suse and their children slept in an attic room of their apartment building during the night, leaving their apartment empty, but by December 1942, they realized that they had to go into hiding for good.

No suitable place that could take all four of them was found, but a childless, non-Jewish couple was willing to accept the children, now aged six and three. The children were drilled into a new identity, hiding the fact that they were Jewish, while Ernst and Suse eventually found a suitable hiding place in the north of Holland.

In Ruth's own words:

*"A lady in the neighborhood, not Jewish but married to a Jew, worked for an underground organization that helped Jews. She found a family to take us, a couple who could not have children of their own, and were consequently content to look after us. In December 1942, my parents took us to them. I was forbidden to tell anyone that I was Jewish and was given a new name – Rudy Klein (my mother's maiden name). Furthermore, my identity involved being an orphan who had lost her parents in the Rotterdam bombing. My brother and I were quite settled with our new family, whom we called Tante Annie and Oom Wim.*

*All was well until September 1943 when the Germans came to the door. Informants had told them about us. We were all forced to accompany them to the police station for interrogation. Tante Annie was imprisoned, and Karel and I were sent to the children's department of the Joodse Schouwburg, the collection point for the Jews. Jewish nursery nurses looked after the children, and one of these had been our nurse at home. This made me feel much better.*

*The girl told me late one night to get dressed quickly. She took me to the sandpit outside to hide. "Sit here till I call you, and don't be frightened," she told me. After the SS had counted the children, she came for me. A network of young non-Jewish students, whose aim was to save Jewish children from transportation to the death camps, spirited children away at night. A student came to take me to the railway station and on to a train to Limburg, in the south of the country. Unfortunately, my brother Karel had become ill with polio and had to stay behind."*

Thus Ruth was picked up one night and she disappeared. Karel had come down with polio and he was probably too small to be "put out" like that. He was eventually "adopted" by a Jewish lady from Borken, our hometown, a distant relative who herself had two children, just before she and her whole family were deported. None of them survived.

I was made aware of this story, about three weeks after the end of the war, at the time when I visited The Hague to check on the arrangements for the return of the Dutch Jews from Terezin. Later that day, I stopped at the home of the sister of the lady who had "adopted" Karel. At that time, Ernst and Suse were still looking for Ruth. They had found some of the women who had worked in the children's department of the Schouwburg, who steered them to some of the men from the underground who had been involved in these rescue missions.

Here is Ruth's story:

> *"In Limburg, I was placed with a Roman Catholic couple who had two children of their own, and were expecting another. Two weeks later, I too contracted polio and had to be admitted to the hospital. The medical director there was told in confidence that I was Jewish. I was very sick, and partially paralyzed. The young man who had brought me to Limburg came to see me and brought me six eggs – a great luxury, as food was strictly rationed, even in the hospital. (After liberation, I was most sad to learn that this brave young man had been caught and executed.)*
>
> *Two and a half months later, I was discharged from hospital, but was homeless, as my former family were too afraid to have me back. The underground movement*

*returned me to Amsterdam where I was accommodated in a home for mentally handicapped children. The matron hid a number of Jewish children who were kept in a separate room. We were of similar age, and despite our young years, helped with general household chores. I was very unhappy and so alone.*

*On the 5th May 1945, the war ended. Despite this, my loneliness increased. Other parents and relatives came to claim their children, but my parents did not appear. We had lost all contact with each other when Karel and I were taken away from Tante Annie and Oom Wim."*

For Ernst and Suse, the trail was cold after having talked to some of the ladies who had worked in the Joodse Schouwburg. The only choice left to them was to contact any family, any organization which was rumored to have saved Jewish children. One day, after visiting a lot of different leads in Amsterdam, they decided to visit one more home for mentally handicapped children, which had not really been recommended, but was the sort of place where the underground might have placed Jewish children. They described Ruth to the Headmistress of that home. That lady pompously demanded official proof of their relationship to any of the children she might or might not house. But secretly, she had given orders to let Ruth come into the room unannounced and Ruth, by now nine years old, who had not seen her parents for three years, spontaneously and joyously recognized her parents.

After the war, Ernst and Suse courageously had another child. That is Marcel Gans, the ex-Mayor of Elqana in Israel.

## Military Government

In the fall of 1945, the Marine Commandos went back to Great Britain for deployment in the Far East. 41 R. M. Commando was actually sent to Hong Kong; but we who spoke German were encouraged to seek other jobs in the army of occupation in Germany. I went to see the military commandant of the part of the Ruhr district in which we were at the time. He asked me to transfer immediately, since he had no German-speaking officers in his command. And so I became one of the three officers who were running the town of Gladbeck, and I was promoted to Captain.

The military government Mayor was a Canadian major. The other member of our three-man team was a very competent, very low-keyed British police officer (i. e., he was a police officer, not just a sergeant). It was his job to rebuild the local police, the local judiciary organization and to fight crime.

I spent the first few days and evenings reading endless memos and letters to find out what I was supposed to do. Then I organized all these papers into systematic files. After that, I felt ready for work.

We set up a local housing administration to deal with the endless disputes about the very limited available housing. Those who had space were forced to sublet. We had to purge the local food rationing authorities of Nazis, and we had a very difficult time setting up a public health system: the local doctors were just too busy in their own practice and did not want to be bothered with public health, but school children had to be inoculated and hospitals had to be rebuilt and reorganized.

Trade unions, political parties and youth groups were being formed, and I attended a lot of their meetings as an observer.

In all this work we had the guidance of military government experts, who, for our district, had their headquarters in Munster. Some of these experts were very helpful. The health expert was a British doctor, an ex-German Jew, and we really needed the legal experts, but a lot of the other experts were just a bunch of bureaucrats, "standing in our way while we were trying to win the peace" (to paraphrase the dictum of the fallen Three Troop member, Peter Moody).

All day long, we were besieged by people who wanted favors. The word spread in Borken that I was in Gladbeck, and several people came to see me to get the release of relatives or to get their "denazification".

Again, we lived in pretty good houses outside the town, drove in requisitioned civilian cars which were none too reliable, and we had four horses which had to be ridden regularly. The Major who had "hired" me had "imported" a young French girl, his mistress, who ran the German cooking and cleaning staff. Tom, the Canadian town mayor, had "tied up" in North Germany with a Lithuanian woman who had been educated in the U. S. She ran our office staff, all of whom spoke and typed English pretty fluently.

One morning, I came to the office with John, the British police officer, when the usual throng of people was waiting outside our offices to get interviews, John remarked, "The small man toward the end of the line is the only surviving Jew of this town." I called him into my office; that was how I met Mr. Kahn. I told him who I was. He was stunned; he had heard about a British Jewish officer originally from this area, who had come to Terezin to find his parents and he just could not believe that it was I.

Kahn was married to a non-Jewish woman. His brother-in-law was a very knowledgeable mine inspector, who hid Mr. Kahn in an abandoned coal mine for almost three years, but Kahn was a restless man; he just had to get out from the underground mine occasionally. When the Allied bombs were falling on the Ruhr district, in the blacked out nights, he wandered the deserted streets, accepting the bombs as Manah from Heaven. One night someone recognized him and word spread like wildfire: "Da ist noch ein Jude". The whole town turned out to find him, but he was back underground. All this time, his wife was in prison, where there were no air raid shelters during bombing attacks. The Nazi authorities would not believe that she did not know where her husband was. She was a nervous wreck when American troops liberated the town, and she insisted that the prison staff be arrested for inhuman behavior.

One of Mr. Kahn's first request to me was to get him a Talith and Tefilin, which my friends sent me from England. Mrs. Kahn was an outstanding cook and I visited them frequently for Shabbat meals.

## The Catholic Church

We became aware that the Catholic Church was preaching that ordinary Germans needed to feel no guilt for the atrocities committed by the Nazis and, this idea originated with the Bishop of Muenster, Bishop Galen, whose anti-Nazi record was impeccable, as I knew only too well from before the war. Colonel Spottiswood, who was the military government commander for the whole Muenster Region, came to have dinner with us one evening and said that he was going to "have Bishop Galen on the carpet" the next day. What should he tell him?

I told him the story of Mr. Kahn and how the whole town turned out to chase him. I also told him to ask the Bishop how he explained that 30,000 Jews were hidden by six million Dutch people, while only 5,000 Jews were hidden by 66 million Germans.

## The Swedes

We accepted an offer from a Swedish organization to set up a soup kitchen and some basic medical supplies for the really poor in our town, and we were joined by a detachment of four Swedes, two men and two women. After they had established their stations, we had an opportunity for many discussions with them. The men actually were officers of the Swedish army. Seeing the destruction in the Ruhr district, they felt that our war had been unnecessarily destructive and that our military government was excessively harsh.

I was in a good position to refute their arguments: they had done none of the fighting. Pinpoint bombings had been conducted quite successfully against a Ruhr target in daylight early in the war, probably just to prove that it was impracticable. From then on, factories, mines, and generating stations were destroyed by night carpet bombing. We had done some very costly street fighting in France, where the population was on our side. Neither the Allied High Command nor we, the troops who had to do the fighting, were willing to subject ourselves to such risks in a hostile population: towns which resisted, like my home town, Borken, were set alight by fire bombs and then destroyed by high explosive bombs.

I introduced the Swedes to my parents when they visited Amsterdam.

In the spring of 1946, a political decision was made by the British government that the military government in Germany should be free of ex-Germans. They probably wanted to demonstrate that they had confidence in the emerging German political leadership of Schumacher and Adenauer. Roger Kingsley and I then spent two weeks in a holding camp near Bielefeld where we did a lot of good horseback riding.

**Captain F. Gray in Zandvoort, Holland**

# Preparation for the Nuremberg Trials

I then became the Deputy Commander of the Intelligence Section attached to a prisoner camp for high-ranking Nazis in the Sennelager near Paderborn. The commander was one of those legendary British Intelligence/Secret Service officers, but he had tied up with a German woman and we only saw him during office hours.

The camp housed 10,000 men and 2,000 women. It was the main task of the Intelligence Section to prepare some of the prisoners for the Nuremberg Trials. Krupp von Bohlen Halbach and one of the ex-Commandants of Auschwitz, Aumeier, were among our prisoners. We worked like blazes, each of five German speakers dealing with about eight cases a day.

Occasionally, American high-ranking officers would visit us, and we had to produce relevant members of the Gestapo and the Sicherheitsdienst to get information on the Nazi spy network in the US.

At one time, we were ordered to interrogate all those who had been involved in the attempted killing of Hitler in July, 1944.

We had a group of a few hundred high-ranking German officers who had spent the war in Norway. They let it be known that the stories of Concentration Camp cruelties and mass killing were not true.

We got Mr. Aumeier, the ex-Auschwitz Commandant to give them a lecture (we had told Aumeier, a common murderer, who joined Hitler in the 20's, that he had nothing to fear since he was only obeying orders of Himmler and such like). The effect on the ex-Norway German officers was devastating. (Many years later I saw a film, Judgment at Nuremberg, where a similar scene is portrayed.)

We found high-ranking Nazis who had committed horrible crimes in Russia, but the Russians were not interested in them.

Each interrogation of a prisoner had to start by filling in a very lengthy "Fragebogen," questionnaire. I got myself a typewriter and typed all the answers. I pretended to be totally preoccupied with the typing. Invariably, the prisoner's Geltungsbeduerfnis made him give more extensive answers. Then I would shoot some very specific, telling questions, giving me a clear picture of the prisoner's past and deeds.

Once, we were visited by a delegation from the British Parliament, who strongly objected to our holding the ex-leaders of German industry. It was my task to argue with Beverly Baxter, a Conservative Member of Parliament, and the editor of the Daily Express. He said, "What if we would treat our own industrial leaders this way?" I answered, "These industrial leaders used slave labor; we mobilized our women to a degree the world has never seen. Remember that book 'Daylight on Saturday'?" The argument went on and on; he was not convinced. Almost a year later, when my girlfriend Anita had come to England, I arranged for Beverley Baxter to let us witness a debate in Parliament. He was very nice to Anita, and we met Anthony Eden, but our argument about the German industrialists continued right there. I suppose that is the purpose of Parliament.

The Sennelager was a fascinating legal, political and psychological experience, worth a book on its own.

In August, 1946, I returned to England for "demobilization". I left the Army on a Saturday night and started working for a competitive University entrance examination on Sunday morning. Within 24 hours I was transformed from a captain in an Army of Occupation who had his own car and plenty of servants, into a student of very limited means, bent on a professional career, which eventually would be even more fascinating than my army experience.

# Student Years

In October, 1946, I entered the College of Technology of Manchester (England) University. There were 80 students in the class, 77 ex-Servicemen and three high school "kids" (two girls, the only female component of the class, and one boy). The university had decided to limit the Intermediate Class to 80 students, but there were 120 applicants. The 80 freshmen were to be chosen from the results of the special two-day examination, for which I started to prepare myself the morning after I left the army. But unbeknownst to us, only 77 ex-service men turned up for the examination, so all of us who turned up passed the examination, which had been so hard that most of us were sure we had failed.

The examination made me miss the funeral of the father of my friend, Roger Kingsley (Otto Loewenstein). I had known Roger before the war; we met again in Three Troop 10 Commando. He agreed to go to an Officer's Training School just before D-Day and rejoined us only after the Walcheren operation. The two of us had to leave military government on the same day, when it was decided that no ex-Germans should serve in the military government. We spent a week or two in a holding camp in Bielefeld before being assigned to different prison camps for high-ranking Nazis.

The average length of military service of the veterans in the University class was five years. I lived in a rented room; it was primitive, cold, and food was bad and scarce. That was all I could afford, though I got the highest ex- servicemen grant in the class.

I had reverted to my original name on the evening I left the army, without any legal papers or paying any fees. "No fuss, no muss, no bother;" nobody ever questioned me on it.

These were the days of the original Labor Government; food was cheap, but severely rationed. The notoriously primitive British cuisine as practiced in the university cafeteria, the cheap restaurants and my private "digs" ensured that eating would be no joy at all. To top off this dismal picture, the winter of 1946/47 was one of the coldest winters on record in Great Britain, while fuels in the form of oil or coal were also severely rationed. Houses were heated by inefficient, open fireplaces; coal rationing assured that only one of these antiques could be kept in operation in every home.

College was tough: I found it very hard to keep up with the rate at which we were supposed to absorb mathematics, physics and chemistry. The mornings were crammed with lectures; the afternoons were spent in laboratories; evenings were needed to write up notes, to make sense of the lectures and to work on textbook exercises. I rarely went to bed before midnight. Of the 77 veterans in the class, about 15 hoped to get a degree in Chemical Engineering, but after four years, I was the only one from that original group who "made it." All the others converted to a general chemistry degree, which was easier to get. Each year, we were joined by groups of students who had obtained high school degrees and/or spent a year or two at universities before their military service, so the class was getting younger as we went along. Also, most of these newcomers were very gifted and well trained. The university could afford to be selective, so competition grew fierce.

I belonged to the university cross-country team, and after working in the lab on Saturday morning, we were in cross-country races in the afternoon. The famous British university debates frequently were a stimulating change during lunch hours.

I did not "date" girls, another drastic change from being an officer in the Army of Occupation, where German women, displaced persons and British service girls, including nurses, could be found easily.

Two quick day trips to London finally qualified me for British citizenship and a British passport, so that I could visit my parents in Holland during the Xmas break.

## Anita-Interlude

I first met Anita when she was ten and I was eleven, in the summer of 1933, on the Hachshara farm, Gut Neuendorf, which was run by my uncle Alex Moch. Since our fathers had been friends at age 16 and 14, when they were both apprentices in a textile business in Frankfurt am Main, I had known about Anita Lamm's existence most of my life.

In 1933, my cousin Bernard was very keen on Anita, but I was quite indifferent. Thereafter I spent some time in Neuendorf every summer until I left for England in 1938, and we usually stopped at the Lamm's house in Berlin on our way back home to Borken.

Shevuoth, 1938, we were again in Neuendorf and Anita and her parents came to see us. My uncle Alex persuaded Anita to try horseback riding under his guidance, and she went for it enthusiastically, though she had never tried it. Of course, I could not join because I was orthodox and it was Shevuoth.

At 15 years of age, she was an accomplished young lady. She had spent a year in a Jewish boarding school in Switzerland, spoke French and English (having spent a summer in England with a very "English" family), played the accordion, had skied in Switzerland and loved sports.

That evening, Shevuoth, 1938, there was some sort of a soiree in the dining hall of Gut Neuendorf, and Anita and I sat on the steps leading to the hall. We talked and commented on the program, and something "lit up" in both of us, as we agreed much later in life.

A few weeks later, Anita spent a weekend with us in Borken on her way to the USA. On that Sunday, she was joined by her father. Ostensibly, they were on their way to Paris for a haute couture (dress) show. Leo Lamm had persuaded the American Consul in Berlin to give him visas to the US in the form of a letter, NOT in the passport, so that the Nazis would not know that he was leaving for good, while he pretended to be buying model clothing in Paris.

That Sunday afternoon my father hid the letter visa in his artificial leg and went across to Holland to his cousin in Winterswijk, who mailed the letter to Paris. A few days later, Anita, her father and her mother, who joined them from England, were off to the US on the Normandie.

That weekend, Anita and I fell in love, hopelessly - and we have the pictures to prove it.

Soon thereafter I left for England. Anita and I corresponded across the Atlantic about once every two weeks, first in German then in English. After about a year, her parents stopped "that nonsense"; among other things, they could not see their daughter committing herself to a totally "unproven" person at that early age.

By the time I was in the Commandos in 1943, I started getting letters via my brother Teo (who did not know where I was) and my cover address, the Wislickis in Manchester, from a totally unknown American girl. Initially I did not answer: before joining the Commandos, while still in the Pioneer Corps, we had been in correspondence with a group of American women, who had sent us some beautiful handmade khaki pullovers, and I thought one of those ladies had just wished to start a more personal correspondence.

But the letters from "Joan" kept on coming and eventually I answered them. Sometime in 1944, I suspected that my correspondent knew more about me than she admitted. Finally, in the winter 1944/45, she sent a picture of herself, eliminating all doubts. I did not give her my cover name or my military address, but I had told her already before D-Day that I was a paratrooper and was leading a very adventurous life. Even after she had revealed her true identity, she insisted on using her assumed name, since she still did not want to admit to her parents that she was in correspondence with me. Only after I sent her my Theresienstadt story in May 1945, did she inform her parents of her secret scheme.

After the war, Anita tried to join one of the relief agencies which were operating in Europe, but she did not succeed. I had planned to "hitch a ride" to the USA on the air ferry service between discharge from the army and joining the university, but then I had to prepare myself for that University entrance examination.

We both realized that somehow we had to "break it or make it," so I invited Anita to come to England during the University Easter break, 1947, and we would then go to Holland together for Pessach.

Anita came over by boat and I met her in Southampton, when she was checking through customs. We then spent a weekend in London before going to Holland to be with my parents in Zandvoort for Pessach.

All that time, I had to spend at least 6 hours a day studying to become more proficient in the multitude of subjects which had been "thrown" at us. To be allowed to go on to Chemical Engineering I had to pass the end-of-the- year examination with "honors." Nevertheless, Anita and I had a very interesting time together: we went dancing in Amsterdam some evenings, biking along the beach, where most of the W. W. II German fortifications were still in place and where all houses within 300 meters of the beach had been torn down to allow free fire zones

Theo also came over for Pessach, and we had a very emotional first, post- war Seder at home.

On our return to England, we stopped again in London for a few days, where I introduced Anita to my friends, including Beverly Baxter in Parliament. In drab, rationed England she stood out by being dressed very tastefully in understated but imaginative, high quality clothes. She surely impressed the Members of Parliament we met. We then returned to still more drab, heavily bombed Manchester.

(Since we were both profligate writers, details of the above story can be found in our letters to each other and the letters to our parents, most of which have been preserved.)

The parents of Anita's friend, Eva Frank, had asked Anita to look up the Chief Rabbi of Manchester, Dr. Altmann, who had been a Rabbi in Berlin in the synagogue where Mr. Posen, Eva's father, had been the president. Anita was amazed that I had been a friend of the Altmanns since 1939, when they first came to Manchester, and that I was very close to their children. Soon, she spent a lot of time with the Altmanns, and the children had no difficulty switching allegiance from me to Anita. As Dr. Altmann said in his speech at Dany's Bar Mitzvah: "Anita's coming to drab, bombed-out Manchester was like the sun finally breaking through gray, depressing, rainy clouds."

We got engaged Shevuoth, 1947. Theo came for the party, which the Wislickis threw for us.

A few weeks later, I took the Intermediate Examination and did well enough for Professor Kenner, the head of the chemistry department, to reluctantly allow me to switch to the Chemical Engineering course, an Honors course. Kenner strongly believed that the future of civilization depended on organic chemistry and that talented students should stay with organic chemistry and not waste their time on learning to design the pots and pans of the chemical Industry.

At the end of the term, Anita and I spent a few days in Aberdovey and we went hiking in North Wales to acquaint Anita with the beautiful areas where we had trained as Commandos, a change of atmosphere from Manchester, prior to my return to college for a very difficult two-week summer course.

During that time, I got myself a summer job as a machine repair fitter with Monsanto in Ruabon, North Wales, my first experience with large-scale chemical equipment. On my way from the job interview in Ruabon, racing from a bus terminal to the railway station through the very picturesque shopping district of Chester, I ran into my only serious ex-girlfriend, who now turned out to be married. Anita was highly

319

amused when I told her about that encounter, but was happy that it provided a "closure" for me.

When we moved to Ruabon, Anita found a farm where we could live, pretending to be married; "cohabitation" was not acceptable in that area at that time. Doing our own cooking was a major benefit of this arrangement. Eventually, Anita drove the tractor for the farmer during harvesting. With the rebuilding of Great Britain in full swing, there was a terrible shortage of labor; anyone willing to work could get any job. No questions were asked about permits or nationality. Anita had the great advantage that she could drive a car, a skill still relatively rare in Great Britain at that time.

Weekends we hiked in beautiful North Wales, or we played tennis on public courts.

One weekend, we went by train to York to visit my father's cousin, Jack Gans, and his wife, Annie, a very well-to-do family who had been very good to the Gans family's, British, Dutch and American soldiers during the war and who were now keen to meet Anita. Jack, as I mentioned before was an outstanding Dutch businessman and Annie, who had been a German opera singer administered their factory. They lived in a beautiful estate very close to the center of York and were highly respected, even by the famous Bishop of York.

In 1944 when my brother Theo, finished High School Jack and Annie had arranged for Theo to start to work for an outstanding German Jewish farmer who had emigrated to England in 1934, had set up an exemplary farm near York and had organized many of the local farmers into a very successful Purchasing and Sales Cooperative.

Towards the end of the war I had "fallen out" with Annie, because I would not provide food packages for her non-Jewish friends and family in Germany. Providing such food packages to civilians was strictly prohibited in the British Army; I was willing to take risks for Jews, but I was not willing to risk my military career for non-Jews. But in 1947, my father visited Anita and me in Manchester before visiting Jack and Annie, (and Theo), and since he could be very persuasive, he straightened out my relations with Annie.

We returned from our summer stay in Ruabon to Manchester at the end of September. Soon thereafter, Anita departed for the USA. We had made up our mind that we would get married the following summer in the USA, that we would honeymoon there, that we would return with some really good furniture (unavailable in post-war England), and that I would organize a pleasant, affordable apartment, so that we would not have to start our married life in a slum.

Once more, we corresponded at least once a week, once more, I had to work very, very hard to keep-up in college, where our class had been joined by a lot of gifted, well-trained, younger students.

At the end of the term in July, 1948, I sailed by the Polish liner Batory to New York. These were the days of the setting up of the State of Israel; the ship was full of GI brides, Jewish emigrants and young US business and relief organization representatives. Debates on Israel and the upcoming US election (we watched bits of the Democratic Convention on TV!) could become furious.

The Batory arrived in New York harbor late one evening, and it had to anchor overnight approximately where the Verrazano Bridge is located now. Initially, it was foggy and we could see only the Belt Parkway, but then the fog lifted and the overwhelming view of the downtown Manhattan skyscrapers and the Statue of Liberty revealed itself.

Next morning, it was hot, humid and rainy; we sailed up the Hudson to midtown. As the ship made its right turn into a pier, I saw Anita standing at the head of the pier, looking super fit and tanned (the result of having exercised with Rosel Kolberg for more than half a year).

Anita and her father met me at the pier with their brand new car. It was hot and humid and I was struck by the fact that all the non Americans who disembarked from the ship were dressed in heavy, totally unsuitable clothing.

Back in England, a friend who was about to marry into as very prestigious but complicated family, had remarked : "You are lucky, you are going overseas to meet you future in-laws, but you have known most of them for a long time". Anita's father had visited us frequently when we still lived in Germany because he and my father had been good friends ever since they worked in the same textile trading company in Frankfurt as teenagers. Anita's mother had visited us only once, but we had stopped regularly in their house in Berlin when we returned from vacations spent on my uncle's agricultural training farm.

We drove to 801 West End Ave, the Lamm's seven room apartment and there was Anita's sister Lilo. Until Anita came to England, I had really spent more time with Lilo, who had stayed at least twice in our home in Borken, than with Anita.. Now, Lilo was heavily pregnant.

Lilo's husband Norbert, the only member of the family whom I had not met before, came for lunch. He was brilliant and always ready to tell some jokes so it was not difficult to warm up to him.

I had arrived on a Tuesday; a few hectic days of meeting family and friends, getting a beautiful grey suit in Uncle Sally's store in the Wall Street area of Manhattan, and we got married in Rabbi Hahn's study, with barely a male Minyan, on Saturday evening. I had known Hahn before the war in Germany. He said, "The story of you two proves that life is much more dramatic than fiction, and the love of parents which you have shown by your trip to a concentration camp has assured that your conjugal love would also be realized."

This ceremony was followed by a reception in the Lamms' apartment. Anita would not allow her parents to spend money on a big, formal wedding, but she wanted their brand new car for our honeymoon trip. All the food for the reception had been prepared by my mother-in-law and her friend, Ruth Wolf. There were 100 people in the apartment. It was hot and humid; air conditioning was not used in private homes yet, but the heat did not bother me, because I, too, was super fit.

My parents had sent to Anita a list of family and friends whom they suggested be invited. All these I had not seen for ten years or more, so the wedding reception became a reunion too.

With the party still in full swing, Anita and I slipped into less formal clothing in Anita's tiny "maids" room behind the kitchen, gathered our belongings, and stole off in that beautiful new car. Some people tried to follow us, but Anita headed for Central Park, stepped on the gas and shook them off. We spent the night in the Barbizon Plaza on Central Park South, luxuriating in the shower, room service food and a view over Central Park.

Next morning we were off, heading north on the Merrit Parkway, for me a stunning impression of a neat, generous layout, luscious vegetation of well tended bushes, trees and grass, attesting to a climate and human organization which I had never imagined.

That night we spent in the bridal suite of the Sturbridge Inn, fully recuperating from the mental strain of the previous week, mixing with fellow guests at dinner and lunch. For me, the food was not only extraordinarily good, but portions were far too large.

The following day, we visited MIT in Cambridge, Mass., at that time the world's leading engineering school. Towards the end of the war, in England, I had become friendly, through the Wislickis, with Professor Sidney Goldstein, the head of the Applied Mathematics Department in Manchester University. He and his wife were ex-South African; later he became the Head of Technion in Israel, before settling in Harvard. Goldstein had tried to get me into Cambridge University in England, but Cambridge didn't have a Chemical Engineering course at that time. But he strongly advised that the combination of an undergraduate degree in England and a post graduate degree in the USA would assure me of a very solid training.

MIT, of course, was in summer recess, but there were students to guide us. The only "authority" in the chemical engineering department was Professor Hauser, an ex-Austrian, ex-Jew, who was much more anti-Communist than anti-Nazi. Nevertheless, when I told him about my past history, he said, "If you have any difficulty getting in here, let me know and I'll see that you will be accepted." There and then, I made up my mind to go to MIT for a Masters Degree once I had finished my studies in Manchester.

That evening, we drove on to Kennebunkport in Maine, and the next three weeks we had a vacation in grand style, staying in pretty good hotels or motels. We enjoyed the beach in Kennebunkport, toured Montreal and McGill University, sailed and hiked in the Thousand Islands, climbed Mount Washington, New Hampshire, on foot, in shorts, because it was far too expensive to ride up by car. We actually got into a snowstorm on top, but we were so fit we kept running all the time. We enjoyed a good hotel and good swimming in Lake Placid before eventually meeting Anita's parents and my uncle and aunt, Sally and Else, in the Catskills.

Back in the New York City area, we were spending a few days on Fire Island with the Franks, when our nephew, David Goldenberg, was born, and we returned to the city when the temperature "hit" 101 degrees at about 100% humidity.

We returned to England by boat in September. On these leisurely boat trips, we always met some interesting people, with whom, subsequently, we were in touch for many years.

My landlady in Manchester, where I had lived under a "bed and board" arrangement, had offered to remove her furniture from my very spacious, light room and to convert one of her attic rooms, half a flight up, into a kitchen. Before I departed, I arranged for a big closet to be built into my room, wall-to-wall carpeting with a very good wool carpet and conversion of the open fireplace into a slow-combustion stove. In accordance with a design plan which we had evolved during the months while Anita was back home, we brought some magnificent furniture, a couch which converted into a twin bed at night and even some custom-made drapes. Thus we lived in a stunning - for post-war England - room, where we could entertain our friends. The bathroom, cold water only for six days of the week, we shared with other people in the house, but we had brought a fitting so that at least we could take cold showers every night. As my friend Roger Kingsley used to say, "You got to be tough to have a little bit of fun in this country."

**Anita in Aberdovey in 1947, after we got engaged**

**Aberdovey 1947**

**Anita's mother Margaret Lamm nee Falk**

**Anita's father Leo Lamm. Picture taken at the
Western Wall in Jerusalem ca 1975**

**Anita's sister, Lilo and husband Norbert Goldenberg.**

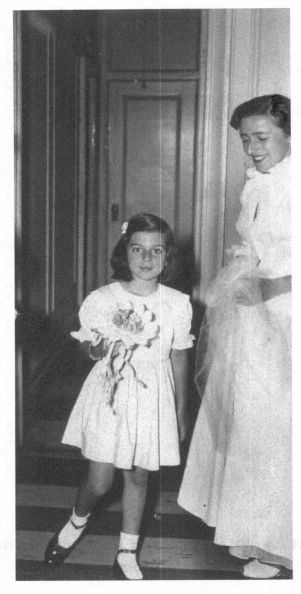

**Wedding 17 July 1948. The flower girl is Eva Lynn
Goldenberg, now Eva Lynn Gans.**

# Three More Years of Studying

Anita got herself a job as a secretary in a very old-fashioned factory which made printing machinery. I went back to my routine of lectures, laboratory work, library studies, rewriting lectures and solving textbook problems. There was never any assigned homework: you had to be totally self-motivated. At the end of each term, we were faced with incredibly difficult tests, including tests in analytical and synthesis laboratory work.

For the examination in each subject I summarized all my notes and then learned the summaries by heart, walking the streets near our home. This was the year in which I broke "the sound barrier" into organic chemistry: suddenly it all made sense, and I got a feel for predicting the outcome of reactions.

At the end of the year, summer 1949, Anita gave up her job, and I took a summer job in a coal gasification/ metallurgical coke production plant in Belgium. I shared the work with another chemical engineering student from the Imperial College in London. We were not allowed to work in the plant, but were assigned research, design and laboratory tasks. Exposure to the laboratory and research staff of the plant was the main benefit of the job.

We lived with Else and Marcel Rotschild in Brussels. Marcel had rented a room from the Lamms in New York during the war; Else, who was not Jewish, had worked for the Belgian government in Washington. They had two children, and Anita helped take care of them. The food was incredibly good, particularly when we were invited to eat with Marcel's parents, who lived in another apartment in the same building. Marcel's brother was a Belgian diplomat, who predicted that, contrary to our idealistic views, the relinquishing of colonial power would lead to utter chaos in Africa. These were the days of the incipient European Union being launched by the creation of the European Steel Union, headquartered eventually in Brussels. Two of my ex-prisoners from the Sennelager prison for high ranking Nazis were among the main motivators, and I did not like it at all.

After six weeks in Brussels, we spent some time with my parents in Holland. By now, they and my grandmother were living in a newly built townhouse near the beech in Zandvoort, and Father was working for my cousin, Karl de Leeuw, in Amsterdam.

Back to Manchester for my senior year. Anita took a job in a textile firm, where the atmosphere was warm and friendly.

My courses now consisted largely of chemical engineering design subjects, with some higher mathematics and surface physical chemistry thrown in to maintain a high scientific standard. This mode of teaching, whereby all chemical engineering design courses were thrown into just one year, was abandoned later because it did not lead to a mature knowledge, and it caused too many students to fail. But we had to suffer through it.

The Wislickis immigrated to Israel, and we took care of some of their affairs; the Altmanns visited Israel for three weeks while we stayed with their children, but there was a housekeeper in the house to cook and clean while we went to work. Roger and Valerie Kingsley were married while we were in Belgium. They set up an apartment in a house opposite us. Roger had graduated that summer. He was one year ahead of me because he had graduated with a high school certificate before the war. He now worked for a petrochemical company founded by two famous Austrian Jews.

I applied for a graduate course at MIT and was accepted long before I graduated in Manchester. MIT had some sort of quota for European students, but few people had the money to pay for tuition and living expenses. I had enough money to pay for the first term and relied on being able to borrow money for the second term, while Anita earned enough money for our living expenses.

I graduated in June, 1950, in a colorful cap-and-gown ceremony. One of those sensation packed, Manchester evening papers featured a front-page story on me and my good-looking wife. Well, to paraphrase my former Prime Minister, Winston Churchill, whose decision to create X Troop had been a major factor: "my life had already been long and not uneventful."

We shipped off our furniture, gave up our apartment and went once more to Holland, where my grandmother had recently died, to meet our sister-in-law, Yael, for the first time, and still more importantly, our three year old nephew Giora. My father was absolutely delighted with his first grandson, and we all had to learn a lot of Hebrew that summer.

After two weeks in Holland, we returned to Manchester to pick up our luggage, and then we took a boat from Liverpool to New York, once more meeting some interesting people, with whom we were in touch for many years.

**Formal Dance, Manchester University, Xmas 1948**

**Graduation, Manchester University, 1950**

# M. I. T.

I went to Boston by bus to look for accommodations, but soon found that, contrary to what everybody had been telling us, there was no shortage and no need to book in advance. After a few weeks of living in a pretty primitive temporary accommodation, we found a very nice, two-room, 4th-floor, walk- up apartment on Beacon Street. Initially, we shared it with a young Jewish couple who had rented that apartment and were now waiting for construction to be completed on a brand new apartment. Since we were all so short of money, it was advantageous to share the rent for two or three months. All this was luxury compared with how we had lived in Manchester: the kitchen was much better equipped, we didn't have to share the bathroom with a whole house of tenants, and there was hot water day and night.

Anita found a job as secretary to the CEO of a company which produced baby furniture; a year later, when we moved back to the New York area, she took charge of the New York office of that company, and she worked there until Aviva was born.

For me, the year at MIT was the most thrilling, productive and stimulating year of my life: first and foremost because of the ready accessibility and personal warmth of all the famous professors, whose names I had known from the chemical engineering literature. They were teachers, and not just lecturers. As long as discussions remained focused on a germane professional subject, they were available just about any time.

All the lectures were didactic: the professor would ask a question and then call on any of us to supply the answer If, by any chance, you gave the right answer, the professor would follow up with a question which really shook your confidence in your answer. If you gave the wrong answer, the professor would follow up with questions which gradually led you to the correct answer. If you answered any question with, "I don't know," he would say, "I bet you a dollar to a doughnut (doughnuts cost five or ten cents at that time) that you do know," and he would gradually lead you to the right answer.

The purpose of these challenging procedures was, in the words of "Doc" Lewis, the father of the department, "to train you to solve problems which don't even exist yet." Occasionally, Lewis, who was already past retirement age, would conduct one of these classes himself.

There were three British graduates in the class; one of them was Eddie Rolfe, with whom I am friendly to this day. His wife, Stephanie, worked in the MIT library, very helpful to us; in the absence of an Internet in those days, we still had to do all our research in the library. Well, on the first day of the semester at MIT, these didactic lecturers really put the three British students through the mill. I suppose they wanted to ensure that we had no feelings of superiority.

Again, there was a large percentage of ex-servicemen in the class, some of them had already spent a year or two in industry since getting their BS degree and were now aiming for a PhD degree, so there was a very mature and cooperative atmosphere, which proved most helpful for doing my research project.

I had booked myself for chemical engineering courses only. The central administration objected: I was supposed to take some courses which furthered my "culture", but the departmental professors told me how to get out of that requirement; they appreciated that we ex-servicemen were in a desperate hurry to start earning a living.

Contrary to my experience in England, there were frequent tests in each course, thus getting away from those "do-or-die" final examinations which had been the curse of our British university education. Once you were admitted to the graduate class of MIT, the faculty felt an obligation to shape you into a mature engineer. Those students who had difficulties reaching that stage were persuaded to attend Practice School, where a small number of students, closely supervised by a professor, worked a few months at a time, in US design, production or research companies.

Each Friday afternoon, the faculty and the graduate class assembled to listen to one of the PhD students presenting the basis and the progress of his research. The first time I attended one of these presentations, the student listed about ten differential equations on the blackboard and proceeded to discuss them to show his progress. I couldn't understand a word and felt most unhappy about it, but at the end of the presentation, Professor Gilliland, the most brilliant member of the faculty, got up and said, "You lost me on your second equation, and I have not been able to follow anything since then." There followed severe criticism, telling the student to "come down to earth."

For my own research thesis I chose a problem which Professor Meissner had set out, involving glutamic acid. This gave me the full advantage of my thorough training in organic chemistry, a subject which most of the other students did not dare to touch, and it had the advantage of being backed by an industrial firm, so that I did not have to worry about money for the equipment and services that I required. I made friends with a PhD student, Tom Goodgame, who had been a submarine officer in the US Navy during WWII. These were the days of the Korean War and there had been a raid behind the North Korean lines involving his submarine and my British Commando unit. Tom advised me to write the research thesis first, and only then do the experiments to prove it. That approach forced me to focus on essentials and greatly reduced the amount of work I had to do in the laboratory.

The results I got were startling; Meissner claimed they were impossible, violating the laws of thermodynamics. I gave him my reasons that these results were very much in agreement with the laws of thermodynamics. Always in a hurry, he swore that one of these days he would take the time to teach me real thermodynamics, but I ran some more experiments and proved that he was wrong. That made my name in the faculty: next semester when I wanted to register for Professor Williams' thermodynamics course, Williams said, "I heard all about you; there is nothing you can learn in my course".

In spite of the terrific workload and our subsistence income, Anita and I participated in many social events involving the faculty and students. On Yom Kippur we walked to the joint MIT-Harvard Hillel service at Harvard, and Anita claimed that, for the first time, she really enjoyed an all-Hebrew service.

For Thanksgiving, Professor Vivian invited us and a Norwegian chemical engineering student and his wife. The Norwegians, who had lived through the war in Norway, really appreciated my war history, as did three French students who were from the Ecole Polytechnique. They were as superior in mathematics to the rest of the class, as I was in organic chemistry.

There were receptions for foreign students, and frequently we met fellow student couples for an evening "out"; most of the American graduate students had cars. Anita's parents came for Pessach and we invited Werner Glass, an ex-German Jew who spent the war in Shanghai and who was the most brilliant student in our class, and his fiancée for Seder. It was the first time we had a Seder in our own home.

Tests were frequently set by the course assistants, not by the professors themselves. These assistants would take the problems from published or unpublished research papers, a procedure which occasionally led to some interesting situations. After one of those tests, in a course which Gilliland gave, I had to see Gilliland's secretary, so Gilliland called me into his office and asked me how I had solved the problem set in the tests. I explained to him what I had done, and he said, "Yes, I was going to do it the same way, but then it occurred to me that there is a much simpler way," which he proceeded to explain to me. I doubt there is any other university where the professors have that type of an approach.

I took Hottel's course on radiation. He was another one of those famous men with whose work I was very familiar before I came to MIT. He and Bob Egbert, who later became my boss at Scientific Design, had mapped the radiation spectrum of carbon dioxide and water mixtures, the basis of all furnace, rockets and similar combustion designs. They had done this work on a grant from the U. S. Defense Department during the war when the Defense Department wanted instruments to discover the location of submarines. These submarines operated on diesel engines, which left a, plume of carbon dioxide and water mixture. (Egbert, who was absolutely brilliant, later claimed that he had done all the work for his PhD thesis, while Hottel got all the credit.)

I really appreciated Hottel, a very friendly, modest genius. When I had to present progress on my thesis, he said, "I don't understand the organic chemistry (he was a mechanical engineer), but the equipment you have designed is all wrong," and he proceeded to tell me the principles for the design of the equipment.

Again, the final test examination was set by Hottel's class assistant. I looked at the test and wrote that there was one variable missing to solve the problem. I then proceeded to make an assumption on that variable, launching me into about two hours of mathematical solutions. In the end, I realized that my assumption was not justified. I would have redone all the work, but two buses were waiting to take us to an open air address by David Ben Gurion at Brandeis University.

I never had to regret my decision. Quite apart from the fact that, to this day, I regard Ben Gurion as the Jewish prophet of our days (yes, he was cantankerous and had his faults, but so had the biblical Moses), I got the highest marks for that test because I was the only one who noticed that there was a missing variable.

Hottel then tried to persuade me to go to work for a furnace-design firm which he consulted, but I found that too narrow a field. Subsequently, my thesis advisor, Meissner, suggested that I work for his friends, Ralph Landau and Bob Egbert. We went for a long weekend to New York for the interview with Scientific Design Company, which had ten employees then, including six engineers.

August 7th, 1951, I started working for Scientific Design Company, the end of my student years and, almost to the day, five years after I left the army. At S. D., we had so much work that we worked until 9:30 every night. I never found the time to attend my graduation ceremony at MIT.

Anita stayed in Boston for another two weeks, to give her boss a chance to find a suitable substitute, and I went to Boston every weekend, traveling by night bus only. On one of those trips I emptied my bank account and took my last savings, $120 in cash, with me. On the bus my wallet was stolen, so we truly started our new life from scratch!

MIT Archives

**Entrance to MIT, Cambridge, MA**

MIT Archives

**Prof. E.R. Gilliland**

MIT Archives

**Prof. H.P. Meissner**

MIT Archives

**Prof. H. Hottel**

# Looking Back

It's now more than 55 years since the end of the events I have described. Life moved forward, and continued to offer family and close friends a chance to pursue professional, social and political ideals.

## Parents

My father started to work as a bookkeeper in the Amsterdam office of my cousin Karl de Leeuw, a one-hour commute by electric train and tram. Karl was killed in an airplane accident in Glasgow, Scotland in 1948, while on his way to the USA. Father had no desire to work for Karl's partner; he ceased that activity and concentrated on his own affairs.

A row of townhouses was built along the beach in Zandvoort, where the Germans had torn down all houses to give their guns a free range of fire. My parents and my grandmother moved into one of these townhouses.

It was now also time to start fighting for the compensation for the properties my father had owned in Germany, all of which had been confiscated without any compensation. Father also launched his claim for German social security payments to which he and my mother were entitled, having paid into the system for years. As a wounded veteran of World War I he had received a small monthly compensation but was eligible for additional payments as an invalid, so he filed a claim for these.

Most importantly, my parents wanted compensation for having worked as slave laborers for the Nazis, particularly for my mother, who had worked directly for the SS while in the Terezin concentration camp.

The fight for lost properties and entitlements proved to be complicated and drawn out; the West German authorities initially did not feel compelled to accommodate the victims of Nazism. Bureaucratic stonewalling was their answer to most claims of this type. But during the Nazi period we had regularly received secret support from a civil service administrator in the Borken town administration, Herr Finke. Father re-established contact with Herr Finke the first time he returned to Germany after the war in 1946. At that time I was still in the British army of occupation, and I met father in Borken. He requested that Herr Finke handle most of the paper work and negotiations for the claims. Eventually he also hired a Jewish lawyer who had returned (from England?) to Duesseldorf.

When the West German government of Konrad Adenauer passed the Restitution Act compensating Jewish victims of Nazi rule, meticulous paperwork for claims became even more important. As a result, father became quite an expert on restitution. He subsequently helped family and friends obtain compensation for their lost possessions and abuses.

My parents came to the USA from Holland for the first time in 1952. They stayed with us in our apartment in Fort Lee for two weeks before attending Fredi and Theo's wedding in California. Wherever they went, New York, California and Chicago, they were entertained by devoted friends and relatives. On their way back from California they again stayed with us until Fredi and Theo, who had crossed the US by car, arrived on their way to permanent emigration to Israel.

With two married sons in Israel, my parents decided to emigrate from Holland to Israel in 1954. They bought the top floor apartment of a four story building in Ramath Gan and furnished it with some of the very solid, modern-style furniture they had brought from Germany to Holland. This furniture had been stored with non-Jewish friends while my parents were in hiding and in concentration camp. A large living room balcony, a small kitchen balcony and extensive built-in closets gave the whole apartment a sense of spaciousness and refreshing airiness, and it became the gathering place for their many friends and the ever-growing family.

Mother loved to entertain family and friends by cooking simple, high-quality meals; everyone would sit around talking and discussing for hours.

Once settled, father resumed his fight with the German authorities for restitution and eventually ensured a comfortably financed retirement for himself and my mother, which included several trips to Switzerland and the USA. He used his litigation experience extensively to steer family and friends in recovering property in Germany and obtaining compensation.

Father also became very active in the synagogue, which was just across the street from their apartment building and which he attended every Friday night and Saturday morning. This congregation was an interesting mixture of German and Iraqi Jews, and Father became their treasurer. I loved attending the Saturday morning services of that synagogue; they had no Rabbi so the Torah portion of the week was read by a man in his eighties. His reading and use of the cantillation were perfect, but his rendition was more like talking than singing. I heard "the word coming out of the desert", which is supposed to be the origin of our scriptures.

Starting in the winter of 1973, when my mother had to have a long-delayed major operation, father's health started to deteriorate. The last seven years of his life – he died in 1980 at the age of 95 - were very hard on him, but he was able to participate in the Brith Milah of his first great-grandchild, Gal Kaddar in 1977.

After father's death, mother went into a deep depression, requiring continuous attention. Luckily, the German Jewish Old Age home was just around the corner from my brother's home, and that became her residence until she died in 1982.

## Three Troop No. 10 Inter Allied Commando

Three Troop never fought as a Troop, but there was at least one of us in every raid, every landing, every assault done by Army or Marine Commandos in North and Western Europe and in the British Mediterranean battle areas.

Battlefield interrogation was our biggest contribution to the war. But to do battlefield interrogation you have to be on the battlefield, and that means being exposed to all the dangers of the normal assault troop soldier. Moreover, once the junior officers, sergeants and corporals who had to do the real fighting realized that we could walk into German positions and calmly persuade the Germans to surrender, they were reluctant to attack or patrol without us.

Our casualties and achievements tell the story: out of 87 members of the troop,

19 were killed in battle; one was killed in training;

22 were wounded in battle, seven of them so severely that eventually they had to be invalided out of the army. Four were injured during training so severely that they were either invalided out of the army or could be used only for office duties.

All of us who were in repeated action were slightly wounded at some time. I still have a splinter from a German hand grenade in my cheek bone, and that causes consternation and alarm every time I need a CATSCAN or MRI.

18 became commissioned officers; four of us got our commissions "in the field", without having attended an officers' training school.

4 were taken prisoner, but the Germans never discovered their true identity. Since our dog-tags, the plastic disc which every soldier wears on his body, stated that we were Church of England, the prisoners from Three Troop, were never identified as Jews, unlike some Jewish-American soldiers, who were consequently mistreated.

George Saunders, the fittest, most daring member of the Troop, the ex Outward Bound student, who could walk on a branch of a tree and jump from one tree to another like a squirrel, was taken prisoner in Normandy when he drove into the German lines accidentally. He escaped twice while still in France, but was caught again and finally was taken to a prisoner of war camp in Germany. When he escaped from there, he decided to go East through the German-Russian lines. He ended up in Odessa, where he persuaded the captain of a British ship to take him along to Great Britain

After the war the members of Three Troop, never kept in touch systematically. We were busy embarking on new professions and careers, but there was an informal network; those who had been close friends in the Troop always knew how to find each other. I stayed in touch with Andrew and Mary Kershaw and started to see Peter Masters regularly, when, as a result of the energy crises in the early '70s, I had to go to Washington frequently because we were developing new processes for alternate fuels.

We had a sort of mini-reunion when Colin Anson and his wife visited the USA and stayed with the Masters in Washington. I wrote a report on that get-together and Peter Masters circulated it to all Three Troop members whose addresses he had.

Subsequently, we learned that J. Leasor was planning to write a book about Three Troop, highlighting the Troop's contribution to the invasion of Sicily, and claiming that the Troop had a strong relationship to the Mafia. We tried to disabuse him of that idea, at first politely, but eventually I had to threaten him with a lawsuit if he did not desist from such a calumnious venture.

Shortly thereafter, Leasor informed us that he had learned from Lord Mountbatten, who was the real "father" of our Troop, that one member of our Troop had been taken prisoner just before D-Day and then was taken to Hitler's headquarter for interrogation. Lord Mountbatten had just been killed by a bomb planted on his private yacht (action of the Irish Republican Army?), so there was no way to check what Mountbatten had told Leasor, whose book, Operation Nimrod, was published a few months later.

The correspondence with and about Leasor spurred our decision to organize a Troop reunion just before the 40th anniversary of D-Day in our former headquarters town, Eastbourne. I had been on a United Nations mission to Turkey and my wife Anita met me at the airport in London. We spent an exciting, week-end, talking, visiting our parade grounds and training places and being interviewed in great depth by Ian Dear, whose book was published a few months later. For the first time we collectively admitted that we had done more than our share in the defeat of the German army.

I had no desire, nor the time to go to Normandy: the ceremonies there were to be dominated by Margaret Thatcher and Ronald Reagan whose theatrics I did not enjoy.

There was another Troop reunion in 1994, just before the 50th anniversary of D-Day. I could not attend because I had to go to Japan to negotiate for machinery for a project in Israel.

Peter Master's book, "Striking Back, A Jewish Commando's War Against the Nazis", was published in 1997 by Presidio Press. It is the most authoritative book on Three Troop and it led to the decision to erect a monument for the Troop in Aberdovey, our "birth place."

Brian Grant, now a respected, retired judge, did most of the negotiations with the town. In June, 1999, twenty two of us ex-Three Troopers gathered in Aberdovey for the unveiling of the monument, joined by widows, sisters and children of ex-members who had fallen in battle or had died since the war. This event was covered intensively by the BBC, one commercial TV channel, local newspapers and even a German newspaper. The BBC intended to make a documentary of the history of the Troop; they had interviewed me by trans-Atlantic telephone for 11/2 hours, and they had the script for their documentary ready before we ever came to

Aberdovey. I was interviewed "on camera" for about two hours including a walk along the beach with my son Dany, who had accompanied me together with his wife Linda and their son Dylan.

The inscription on the monument refers to us as "refugees from Central Europe". Peter Masters and I had argued vehemently that it should read "refugees, mainly Jewish, from Central Europe," but we lost that fight. Amongst others, the town authorities felt that any reference to "Jewish" would lead to vandalism.

We all realized that this was the last time we would meet.

A lot has been written about the Troop. I have mentioned Peter Masters' "Striking Back, A Jewish Commando's War Against the Nazis" (Presidio Press 1997). James Leasor's book, "Operation Nimrod," is somewhat fictitious, but is based on George Lane's (an ex-Hungarian who came to the troop already as a Lieutenant) experience just before D-Day, as fully described in a *Sunday Daily Telegraph* article in the summer of 1984. Captain Hilton Jones, the original Troop commander, wrote an official history and assessment of the Troop in 1946, at the end of the war. The book "X Steht fuer Unbekannt, Deutsche und Oesterreicher in den Britischen Streitkraeften im Zweitem Weltkrieg" by Peter Leighton-Langer is very well researched and deals with the stories of Three Troop members extensively.

In 1999, the BBC produced a 90-minute radio play documentary about Three Troop. A TV documentary was proposed and a lot of footage and a "short" were filmed, but the documentary was never funded by the BBC management.

The fact that the script of the documentary had my story as its central theme and that during all these negotiation I was living in Nazereth Illith in Israel, probably did not help to get BBC management approval for this project.

In 2006 Nick van der Bijl published "No.10 (Inter-Allied) Commando 1942-1945, Britain's Secret Commando" (Osprey Publishing). The book contains many well reproduced photographs and attempts to provide a history of each Troop (French, Belgian, Dutch, Norwegian, Polish, and our troop, the "British" Troop). Its emphasis on dress and clothing is a bit disconcerting.

Linda Gans

## Unveiling of Monument for 3 Troop 10 IA Commando. Aberdovey 1999

## Borken

My grandmother's family had lived in and around Borken for centuries. My Dutch grandfather, Karl Gans, suddenly found himself almost penniless when his father, Abraham Gans, had lost his family's fortune on one ill-fated shipment of cows from Holland to England. At that time, Grandfather was already engaged to my grandmother. He offered to annul the engagement, but she persuaded him to move to Borken to start his business life over again. He resumed his trading of cattle, while Grandmother ran a textile store, which they had carved out from one of the rooms next to the entrance of their home. A stable for 3-5 cows was in the back of their home all under the same roof and all within the ancient walls and moats of the town.

Eventually my grandparents would have five sons and five daughters. All their sons were soldiers in the German army during World War I. My father was the only Jew ever elected to the Town Council in the, by now, more than 800 years of the history of this "Free Town" and its equally ancient Jewish population.

The Jewish elementary school, which in its first four grades had trained us in the fundamentals of Orthodox Judaism and which served as our Hebrew school in the afternoons and on Sunday morning once we attended the public high school, was also located within the walls and moats of the town, as were the adjacent synagogue, the mikve (ritual bath) and the school yard.

During the Nazi period, Borken had 8000 inhabitants, including about 25 Jewish families. Essentially everyone knew everyone else. We could not hide, and as the Nazi ideology sunk in, the streets could become dangerous and unpleasant for us.

As related in this book, the unit to which I was assigned just before D-Day, the 41st Royal Marine Commando, was one of the very thinly spread out British or Canadian units containing the German army in Holland. After these Germans had surrendered in May, 1945, 41st Royal Marine Commando was ordered into Germany, and Borken was our first occupation assignment. To this day, few people can believe that I had nothing to do with that assignment; it was completely fortuitous, but it was one more telling event in the relationship of our family and Borken.

While still in the army I visited Borken several times, even after 41st Royal Marine Commando and I had been moved to other assignments. Twice I met my father there to help him in his fight to get compensation for lost properties. Once I came to visit the only one of our Jewish elementary school mates who had survived

Auschwitz. I had run into her at the only Chanukah party for the whole Ruhr area in 1945. Her parents, her three married sisters and their husbands, as well as two brothers, had perished. She was living in Borken awaiting a visa to the USA, where eventually she married and settled in Washington, D. C.

Once I was out of the army I had no more interest in Borken. My professional life repeatedly brought me to Holland, the Ruhr district and Berlin, and for those visits I usually had a rented car, but I never had the desire to go to Borken.

In 1986/87 several of us ex Borkener Jews, now living in the USA or Israel were approached by a lady from Borken who was writing her masters thesis on "The Relation of the (local) Catholic Church and the Nazis." Eventually we saw the result of her research; she took the Church to task for its silence when, amongst other misdeeds, the local Jews in Borken were subjected to ever-increasing harassment.

We then learned that this young lady was a member of the Town Council and that there was a suggestion that the town should invite the surviving ex Borkener Jews to the 50th anniversary of Kristallnacht. In the fall of 1988 we received these invitations: every ex Borkener could bring one spouse or close relative, and the town would pay for one week of hotel stay, as well as all flights and other transportation costs. The town now has 30,000 inhabitants and is very wealthy.

In intensive discussions by fax and telephone between Israel, the USA and Holland, we, the survivors of the former Jewish community of Borken, decided that we would accept the town's invitation only if we were allowed to lecture in all the high schools and middle schools on the Holocaust, on our personal experiences during the Nazi period and on Judaism. These conditions were accepted enthusiastically by the town administration and all the schools.

My late wife and I set out on a Sunday night in early November, 1988, to fly to Duesseldorf, which is about 60 miles from Borken. At the airport in New York we were joined by another couple, distant relatives of mine living in the Bronx, very Orthodox; the husband, about six year younger than me, had been born and raised in Borken. We had always been very fond of this couple. At least, this reunion in Borken would give us a chance to spend time with friends and relatives.

Next morning at 7 A. M local time, we were met at the airport by an official car from the Borken town administration, which had also brought Mechthild Oenning, the young lady whose Masters thesis had set off all these events. She was even younger than I had guessed, quite good-looking, very intelligent and always ready for some light-hearted fun or some very serious discussions.

There were 19 of us ex-Borkeners who returned for this week-long, well organized reunion. Each of us came with a spouse or a close relative, and there was one American-Jewish couple who happened to be in Germany, had heard about this event and was keen to witness it at their own expense. So there were 40 of us, all Israelis and/or well trained Orthodox Jews.

The first night of our stay we attended an inter-faith service led by the local Catholic and Protestant priests and my younger brother, Teo, who lead the Jewish, largely Hebrew, part of the service. This outdoor commemoration, illuminated only by burning torches, took place on the spot where our synagogue and Jewish school had been. About 250 people from the town participated. For the first time in the 800 years of the history of this town our Hebrew prayers and Israeli songs echoed through the still densely built town. Bearing in mind that more than 100 Jews from Borken had been killed in the Holocaust, this night left us with an eerie feeling.

Next morning I lectured in the high school for the first time. The students were totally attentive. I had been assigned two periods of 45 minutes each, but when the bell rang for the intermission, nobody left; pointed questions and lively discussions kept everyone fascinated.

In the afternoon we had been invited to coffee and cake by the members of the Town Council. It was interesting to see that these politicians, who were the generation of our children asked all the same questions as the children had asked in the high school in the morning.

In the evening we attended an indoor Kristallnacht commemoration in a modern auditorium built on top of a municipal building. More than a thousand people were in the audience. Among the speakers was the Chief Magistrate of Borken, who showed, by quoting recent articles and books, that Germany is still not facing its horrendous past. Mechthild Oenning presented a well researched lecture on the 700-year history of the Jews in Borken.

This intensive sequence of events continued during the next six days of our stay. I lectured three more times in different high schools; we had a religious ceremony in the restored Jewish cemetery; we participated in the opening of an exhibition on the history of the Jews in Borken; the two non-Jewish classmates of mine who had never joined the Hitler Youth came to see me. One now is a mathematics teacher in Aachen; the other had become a famous syndicated journalist (He subsequently wrote a very dramatic article about me). We visited our old home, now the home of a film producer/ director.

My wife, Anita, my sister-in-law, Fredi, and I wrote extensive reports for family and friends about these unique experiences. We called the collection of these reports "Kaddish after Fifty Years."

Three incidents illuminate the background and the consequences of this eventful week:

After my brother Teo had given his first talk in one of the high schools, a student was quoted in the local-daily newspaper as saying: "This is what I really wanted to hear. I am not so much interested in what happened in Berlin or in Hamburg, I want to know what happened here in Borken."

One afternoon my brothers and I and our wives were invited to the home of one of the ladies of the Committee for Jewish History. Her 23- year-old son, who was a journalist in another town, was home to talk to us. I described to him the rapid exclusion from classmates and society we experienced after the Nazis came to power. He was stunned and said: "This could not happen today anymore. German youth has changed. Any authority trying such exclusion would face an uprising of German youth. There would be blood flowing in the streets."

The third of these revealing incidents occurred when one of the wealthiest and most influential ladies of the town was driving me to an appointment one late evening in her fancy Mercedes. This lady is about five years younger than me. She was a striking beauty as young girl. I was aware of her when I went to high school, because in a small town like Borken everybody knows everybody else.

On the way this lady related a story which she obviously wanted to tell to one of us "returnees."

In West Germany the history of the Nazi period was never taught. Even high school history books were blank on that subject. Then suddenly, in the mid seventies, it was decided to teach the gruesome truth. One day this lady's two sons came home and screamed: "You are all a bunch of cowards and liars and we cannot live here anymore."

Now suddenly I saw the motivation of all these influential people to reestablish contact with us Jews, formerly residents of Borken. Four times in our Torah there are sentences which start out with the words: "If your sons ask you tomorrow.....and depending how the questions are posed, the Hagada, which we read on Pesach night, divides the sons into four categories: the righteous, the wicked, the simple and the one who is too young to ask questions. But my mentor, Rabbi, Dr. Altmann had taught that the first part of these four sentences "if your sons ask you tomorrow...." is really the more important part, because there we learn that, first and foremost, we have to justify all our beliefs and actions before God and our children.

It took a long time to convince those boys that there was a limit to what individuals could do once the Nazi dictatorship had been established, their mother related.

By the time we left Borken, it was agreed between us and the town administration that

the town would finance a Holocaust memorial monument designed with input from us;

any time the schools would want us to lecture, the town would pay for our transportation and lodging expenses. This is a unique arrangement not found in any other town in Germany.

In the years from 1988 to 2000, our cousin, Herbert Jonas, my two brothers and I regularly returned to Borken to lecture in the high and middle schools. My younger brother, Theo, went almost every year until he died in 1996. I could go only every second year since, I was still too busy professionally, but I could usually connect my visits to Borken with a United Nations mission, so the town did not have to pay for my flights.

In 1990, I gave a lecture on the main principles of Judaism to the combined last two grades of the academic high school as part of their course on comparative religion. The course was normally given by a very intelligent, very devout Catholic lady, who subsequent to my lecture was given a lot of critical arguments by the students. Nevertheless, this teacher and I became very good friends.

I spent half a day with my friend, the journalist, in his home in Muenster and I spent an evening with the hard-working Committee for the History of the Jews in Borken to learn about their plans.

We had decided that on the Holocaust Memorial in Borken the names of the victims from Borken be laid out in the style adopted for the Vietnam Memorial in Washington, D. C. Anita and I drove to Washington and visited the Vietnam Memorial with Peter Masters, who, apart from being the historian of Three Troop 10 IA Commando, also was an outstanding commercial artist. Peter pointed out to Anita the artistic features of the Vietnam Memorial Monument, and Anita then laid out the 100 or so names for the Borken monument on the computer.

Anita died in January, 1991.

We were invited to Borken for the unveiling of the Holocaust memorial monument for a weekend in May, 1992. That weekend happened to be my Bar Mitzvah anniversary, enabling me to read the Torah for the Sabbath morning services. The unveiling was planned for Sunday afternoon, and I was given the honor of speaking on behalf of the Jewish ex-Borken citizens.

My son Dany came along as my companion. We had made arrangements to borrow a Torah from the synagogue in Reklinghausen. We rented a car at the airport in Duessoldorf when we arrived in the very early hours on a Friday morning, and drove to Borken via Reklinghausen. After we had found a suitable place for the Torah in the closet of our hotel room, Dany took the Torah out of the car saying: "Let history record that I brought the Torah back to Borken."

The memorial is set in the ancient walls of the town where these walls overlook the river which was part of the moat of the town and overlooks an ancient Jewish cemetery on the banks of that river.

In my speech, which I wrote only late on Saturday night, I thanked the town for financing the monument and for letting us teach about the Holocaust and Judaism in the schools. In talking about the Holocaust and the lessons to be learned from it, I drew heavily on the views put forward by my late friend, Professor Altmann. I had been able to make a Xerox copy of my speech just a few hours before the ceremony, and I gave that copy to the reporter from the local newspaper, to assure an accurate account.

All the above events and many other dramatic happenings of the1992 visit to Borken I recorded in a special letter to friends and family, as I had done for all the previous visits.

Our almost annual lectures to the schools in Borken continued. My last visit there was in the year 2000. By the year 2002 my health had deteriorated and I was reluctant to subject myself to the hardships of travelling and lecturing. Similarly, my two cousins and my younger brother, who had been part of our lecturing team, had either passed away or were too handicapped to travel. But all those familiar with the fate of the German Jews in the 20th century find this post-50th anniversary of Kristallnacht story of Wiedergutmachung (restoration of good will) amazing and unique.

# Myself

## Professional Career

### Education

B. Sc. Hon Chem. Eng. Manchester (England) 1950

S. M Chem. Eng. M. I. T. 1951.

### Scientific Design Company

I worked for Scientific Design Company for 34 years. I rose from the rank of a Process Engineer to Senior Vice President in Charge of Technology, while the company expanded from a dozen employees to become a major world engineering company.

Having obtained a Master in Chemical Engineering from M. I. T. in 1951, I joined Scientific Design Company in New York City. I was its 11th Graduate employee; eventually we had 700 Graduate employees.

It was the purpose of the company to invent, develop and commercialize new chemical processes. Our research was initially done "on paper". Only when all calculations indicated that a new process was chemically and economically feasible did we start to try it in the laboratory, which was manned by only two chemists when I joined the company.

During the first four years I worked as a Design Engineer, was put in charge of development of physical chemical data, helped out in the laboratory, mainly on night shifts, and participated in the start-up of one major chemical plant.

In 1955 I was put in charge of the company's first pilot plant, while we developed new processes for chemical intermediaries for synthetic fibers and plastics. As result of these developments we became a major player in the international chemical process industry.

In 1957 I became part of the newly formed Operations Department. In the course of the years I personally started up seven novel processes in France, Japan and the US.

In 1963 I became the Assistant Vice President in charge of Operations and in 1965 I became Vice President of Process Design and Operations. Subsequently, I also took charge of the Process Development and Project Engineering departments.

My family and I lived in France twice for a year, for starting up novel chemical plants. Altogether I spent a year in Japan and I spoke some Japanese. In 1967 I spent one week in England every month, I spent time in Rumania,

Poland and the former East Germany, apart from Sweden and every Western European country. I lived in Spain for four months, I went to Australia twice and I negotiated the company's first contract in China in 1973.

In 1973 I was appointed Senior VP of Technology charged with the development of processes which had not been researched in our own laboratory, but which we had acquired from other inventors. My department was on a profit and loss basis: I was given no funds to invest, but had to make enough money through engineering and consultancies to have the department stand on its own legs. The international energy crisis presented us with an opportunity to develop processes for synthetic fuels. Our work was largely paid for by the US government and Utility companies.

In the early 1980's Scientific Design Company and its associated companies were sold to a major natural gas company which wanted to diversify. But the new management bad no idea how to run a research oriented company ("you can't run a gourmet restaurant in New York just because you successfully run a huge cattle range in Texas"). In 1985 the activities of Scientific Design were greatly reduced and I was offered early retirement. The company still exists and is now owned by a German-Saudi consortium.

# Independent Company

On "retirement" I set up my own company, Technology Evaluation & Development Associates, Inc., (TEDA), with two partners and three close associates. We rented our office space from my son Dany. We struggled along for two years but then we became very successful. Work included hazards analyses, technology assessments, plant troubleshooting, expert witness and arbitration, process engineering, pollution abatement and a major project for the production of synthetic fibers in Israel.

United Nations Consultant

In 1978 I had started to become a Consultant to United Nations. By that time I had 5 weeks of vacation and my wife loved to travel. Missions included:

- An Evaluation of Applied Research Facilities in Cuba.
- Setting up an Applied Research Institute for Petrochemical, Plastics and Food Processes in Argentina.
- Chairman of a Technical Assistance Committee for Turkey charged with expanding an Applied Research Institute for Petrochemicals and Plastics.

- Missions to Vietnam, Indonesia, Brazil and Pakistan to advise on creation of specific institutes and industries in the Chemical Sector.
- Chief Technical Adviser for setting up an Applied Research Institute for Refinery and Petrochemical Industry in Pakistan. Visited Pakistan repeatedly.

I am very proud that I lectured for three hours, in the University of Hanoi, Vietnam, to a totally hostile audience in 1987, 13 years before President Clinton faced a similar task.

I was awarded 6 Patents, and am the author of 15 technical papers, published in major trade magazines.

I systematized the fields of chemical plant start ups and trouble shooting and have lectured extensively on these subjects and on Process Engineering.

I have been a Fellow of the American Institute of Chemical Engineers since 1982, and was the winner of the 1993 "Chemical Engineering Practice" Award.

Due to ill health, I essentially ceased professional activities in 2002.

## Personal History Since 1951

1952    Aviva was born, followed by Dany in 1954.

1957    Whole family spent almost a year in France. Visited Israel for the first time.

1958    Spent five month in Japan. Been there repeatedly for extensive stays since then.

1960    Became active in local Jewish Community and local Democratic Party. Anita was already very active in ORT. Eventually became President of Jewish Congregation in Leonia.

1964    Whole family spent another year in France.

1966    First trip to Australia.

1967    Commuted to England once a month, Dany's Bar Mitzwa

1972    Lived in Spain for four months.

1973    First trip to China, East Germany.

1976    First job for the UN in Cuba. Have taken on projects for the U. N. in Argentina, Pakistan, Vietnam, Turkey, Indonesia and Brazil since then.

1985    Avivas's wedding. Happiest Day of our life. Took early retirement from Scientific Design. Set up my own Company TEDA

1988    Emotion packed return to Borken for anniversary of Kristall Nacht. Since then lectured in Borken schools almost every year.

1989    Anita diagnosed with ovarian cancer.

1990    Started work on Spandex project for Israel. Aaron was born.

1991    Anita died. Gradually tied up with Ester Okin whom Anita and I had known for 15 years and whose husband had left her.

1992    Jeremy is born.

1996    Dany gets married to Linda. Dylan is born.

Construction of Israel Spandex project starts and I move into an apartment in Nazareth Illith

1998    Spandex Plant starts up. I am diagnosed with Parkinson Disease.

1999    Commando Troop reunion for inauguration of a monument in Aberdovey Wales, where we had originally trained. Spent 3 months in Israel in Spandex Plant after that.

2000    In Israel for Gershon's 80th birthday and trying to find a new management for Spandex Plant.

2002    Parkinson condition worsens. Ended active professional career.

2003    Moved to an apartment in Fort Lee.

# INDEX